The Language of Leadership

Effective Phrases for Every Scenario

Brent Ziemann

The Language of Leadership

Brent Ziemann

Published by:
Possiblity Institute
3305 Long Prairie Road
Flower Mound, Tx 75022 USA

Typesetting: Brent Ziemann

Cover Design: Brent Ziemann

A CIP record for this book is acailable from the Library of Congress Cataloging-in-Publication Data

ISBN-13: 9798877546103

Printed in USA

Contents

PREFACE

Welcome to a journey through the nuanced landscape of human communication, a journey born from a mosaic of experiences ranging from the boardrooms of corporate America to the dynamic floors of retail sales, and coaching on the spirited fields of basketball and baseball. This book is a culmination of insights gathered not just from theoretical study, but from rich and diverse discoveries from real-life interactions.

As a corporate executive, I navigated the intricate world of leadership and teamwork, where every word carried weight and the art of enrolling was pivotal. It was in the high-stakes meetings and strategic decision-making sessions that I first began to recognize the power of specific phrases and how they could alter the course of a discussion, resolve conflicts, or build unshakeable alliances.

Transitioning to the bustling environment of retail sales, these phrases took on a new dimension. Here, communication was not just about making decisions or resolving internal conflicts; it was about connecting with a diverse array of customers, understanding their needs, and guiding them to satisfactory outcomes. The challenge was to be intentional, empathetic, and effective – often in the span of a single conversation.

Parallel to my professional journey, coaching basketball and baseball provided a unique perspective on communication. On the field, I learned the importance of motivation, the impact of encouragement, and the necessity of constructive feedback. It was here that I realized the immense potential of words to inspire, to teach, and to bring out the best in people.

This book distills the essence of all these experiences. It is not just a guide to effective communication; it is a reflection of the diverse ways in which strategic phrases can be applied across different realms of life. Each chapter is infused with real-life examples and practical advice, drawn from the various hats I've worn throughout my life.

You will find that the phrases and strategies discussed are not confined to any single field. Rather, they transcend boundaries, offering value to anyone, regardless of their profession or stage in life. Whether you are a leader seeking to inspire your team, a salesperson aiming to connect with clients, a coach nurturing potential, or simply someone looking to improve personal relationships, this book offers insights that are both practical and transformative.

As you embark on this journey, I invite you to not just read but to engage with the content. Test these strategies in your daily interactions. Observe the responses they elicit and the impact they have. This book is more than just a collection of words; it's a toolkit for building stronger, more meaningful connections with those around you.

So, let us begin this journey together, exploring the art of strategic communication, and unlocking the potential in every conversation.

CHAPTER I

Resolving Arguments with "Imagine If..."

Welcome to the first chapter of our exploration into the art of creative communication, titled "Resolving Arguments with 'Imagine if...'". This chapter serves as an essential guide to understanding and harnessing one of the most powerful tools in the realm of dialogue and debate: the strategic use of imagination.

In our daily interactions, be they personal, professional, or public, we often encounter situations where we need to create opportunities with others or articulate our perspective effectively. Whether it's convincing a team about a new business strategy, negotiating with a child about bedtime, or debating significant societal issues, the ability to enroll others effectively is invaluable.

The Power of "Imagine if..."

The phrase "Imagine if..." stands out as a unique and potent instrument in the arsenal of enrolling techniques.

At its heart, this phrase is an invitation - an invitation to step into a world of possibilities, to explore potential outcomes, and to consider scenarios beyond the immediate and apparent. It's a prompt that encourages people to visualize, empathize, and connect with an idea on a deeper level.

Why "Imagine if" Works...:

It opens Minds to New Possibilities: When faced with resistance or skepticism, "Imagine if..." helps in breaking down mental barriers and opening up minds to new ideas and solutions.

1. Creates Empathy and Emotional Connection:

By encouraging others to put themselves in different scenarios, it fosters empathy and a deeper emotional connection to the issue at hand.

2. Facilitates Creative Problem-Solving:

This phrase is a springboard for creative thinking, pushing individuals and groups to think outside the box and envision innovative solutions.

3. Overcomes Obstacles:

It transforms perceived obstacles into opportunities for growth and change, reframing challenges in a more positive and manageable light.

4. Engages and Captivates the Audience:

The imaginative nature of the phrase makes discussions more engaging and memorable, capturing the interest and imagination of the audience.

In this chapter, we will explore the various facets of "Imagine if..." in the context of resolving arguments and discussions. Through real-world examples, practical tips, and detailed exploration, we aim to provide a comprehensive guide on effectively using this phrase to enroll, resolve, engage, and inspire.

Join us on this journey to unlock the transformative power of imagination in the art of enrolling, and discover how the simple act of imagining can lead to impactful and positive outcomes in various aspects of life.

Section 1: The Power of Possibility

In the realm of enrolling communication, few techniques are as potent as the artful use of imagination. The phrase "Imagine if..." is a gateway to this realm, inviting listeners to step into a world of potential and possibility. This section delves into the power of this phrase, illustrating its effectiveness with real-world examples.

The Essence of "Imagine if..."

At its core, "Imagine if..." serves as a bridge between the present reality and a realm of potential futures. It's a tool that transforms an argument or discussion from a mere exchange of facts and opinions into an exploration of what could be.

This phrase has the unique ability to shift perspectives, challenge preconceptions, and open minds to new possibilities.

Case Study 1: Transforming Environmental Policy

Consider the case of a small town grappling with the challenge of pollution. Environmental activists struggled to convey the urgency of the situation to local authorities and the public. The turning point came during a town hall meeting when a young activist began her speech with, "Imagine if our town could become a model of environmental sustainability..."

This simple invitation to imagine set the stage for a transformative conversation. It shifted the focus from the overwhelming problem of pollution to the exciting potential of a cleaner, greener future. The audience was no longer mired in depressing statistics about pollution levels; instead, they were envisioning a vibrant community, leading the way in environmental responsibility. This approach not only won the hearts and minds of the attendees but also led to the adoption of significant environmental policies.

Case Study 2: Changing Perceptions in Healthcare

Another illustration of the power of "Imagine if..." comes from the healthcare sector. In a bid to improve patient care, a hospital was considering the adoption of a new, but costly, technology. The decision-makers were hesitant, focusing solely on the immediate financial implications.

It was a nurse, during a staff meeting, who shifted the conversation by saying, "Imagine if this technology could save even one life every month..."

Her words brought a new perspective to the table. Instead of viewing the technology as a financial burden, the committee started seeing it as a life-saving tool. The focus shifted from cost to value – the value of human life and quality of care. This reframing of the issue led to the unanimous decision to acquire the technology, significantly improving patient outcomes.

Case Study 3: Education and the Power of Possibility

In the educational sphere, "Imagine if..." has been used to revolutionize teaching methods. A school district grappling with low literacy rates among students found hope through this phrase. A new superintendent, during a district-wide teacher's conference, posed a simple question: "Imagine if every child in our district could read at grade level..."

This prompted a wave of creative ideas and strategies among the educators. They moved away from traditional, ineffective methods and started implementing innovative teaching techniques tailored to their students' needs. By imagining a future where every child could read, they were motivated to make that vision a reality. The result was a significant improvement in literacy rates and a more inclusive and effective educational environment.

Case Study 4: Business Innovation through Imagination

In the business world, "Imagine if..." has been a catalyst for innovation and growth. A classic example is a small start-up struggling to break into a saturated market. During a brainstorming session, the CEO challenged the team with, "Imagine if we could offer something no other company in our industry does..."

This challenge sparked a flurry of creative ideas, leading to the development of a unique product that addressed a previously unmet need in the market. The company not only entered the market but also set a new standard, all because they dared to imagine a different kind of future for their business.

In each of these cases, the phrase "Imagine if..." opened a door to new possibilities. It encouraged people to think beyond the confines of their current reality, to envision a better, more promising future. Whether it's in environmental policy, healthcare, education, or business, the power of possibility can lead to significant changes and advancements.

By inviting others to imagine, we not only present an enrolling argument but also engage their emotions and intellect in a way that facts alone cannot. "Imagine if..." is not just a phrase; it's a powerful tool for change, a catalyst for innovation, and a beacon of hope in a world that often focuses too much on what is, rather than what could be.

Section 2: Empathy and Connection

In the art of enrolling, creating a bridge of empathy and connection is crucial. The phrase "Imagine if..." is a master key in this endeavor, allowing the speaker to guide the listener into a space of shared discovery and emotional alignment. This section explores the effectiveness of this phrase in fostering empathy and connection through various real-world examples.

The Role of "Imagine if..." in Building Empathy...

Empathy is the ability to understand and share the feelings of another. In discussions and arguments, invoking empathy can be transformative. "Imagine if..." is a powerful prompt that helps listeners step into someone else's shoes, see things from a different perspective, and connect with issues on a more personal level.

Case Study 1: Bridging Divides in Community Conflicts

Consider a community divided over the construction of a new public facility. Tensions were high, with residents split between supporting and opposing the project. A community leader, in an attempt to find common ground, used the phrase, "Imagine if this facility were in your backyard..."

This simple yet profound invocation of empathy allowed each side to understand the concerns and feelings of the other. It shifted the conversation from a debate about land use and regulations to a dialogue about respect, community, and shared values.

This empathetic approach led to a compromise that addressed the concerns of both groups, fostering a sense of unity and mutual respect.

Case Study 2: Humanizing Immigrant Experiences

In the context of immigration policy debates, empathy often takes a back seat. A journalist covering the struggles of immigrants used the phrase "Imagine if you were forced to leave everything you know behind..." in a powerful editorial.

This prompted readers to consider the human aspect of immigration beyond the political rhetoric. It encouraged them to think about the fear, uncertainty, and hope that drives individuals to seek a new life in a foreign land. This empathetic framing brought a new level of understanding and compassion to the issue, influencing public opinion and policy discussions.

Case Study 3: Corporate Social Responsibility

A multinational corporation was facing public backlash over its environmental practices. The CEO, in a speech to shareholders, used the phrase, "Imagine if this were your community being affected..."

This empathetic approach changed the conversation around corporate responsibility. It led to the implementation of more sustainable practices and a commitment to community welfare.

By encouraging shareholders to empathize with affected communities, the company not only improved its public image but also contributed positively to societal well-being.

In each of these examples, "Imagine if..." served as a catalyst for empathy and connection. It encouraged individuals to step out of their own experiences and consider the emotions, struggles, and perspectives of others. This empathetic approach can transform arguments and discussions, leading to more profound understanding, meaningful connections, and ultimately, positive change. Empathy, fostered through the power of imagination, has the ability to bridge divides, humanize abstract issues, and create a foundation for more compassionate and effective solutions. Whether in community conflicts, healthcare, corporate responsibility, or social justice, "Imagine if..." is not just a phrase; it's a tool for building a more empathetic and connected world.

Section 3: Overcoming Obstacles

In the journey of enrolling and dialogue, encountering obstacles is inevitable. Whether these are entrenched beliefs, logistical challenges, or emotional barriers, the phrase "Imagine if..." emerges as a powerful tool to navigate and overcome these hurdles. This section examines how this phrase can reframe obstacles as opportunities, illustrated through three real-world examples.

The Function of "Imagine if..." in Dissolving Barriers...

"Imagine if..." is more than a mere rhetorical device; it's a lens that transforms problems into possibilities. It encourages individuals to envision a reality where current obstacles are surmounted, thus opening up pathways to innovative solutions and mutual understanding.

Case Study 1: Revolutionizing Urban Planning

In a large metropolitan city, the proposal for a new public transportation system faced stiff opposition due to concerns about cost, disruption, and feasibility. The project seemed destined for rejection until a city planner addressed the council with a compelling question: "Imagine if our city could reduce traffic congestion by 50%..."

This simple reframing turned the conversation on its head. Instead of focusing on the hurdles, the council began discussing the positive impacts such a system could have on the city's future. This shift in perspective led to a collaborative effort to find workable solutions, ultimately resulting in the successful implementation of the transportation system, drastically improving the city's traffic flow and quality of life.

Case Study 2: Transforming Educational Policy

In a rural district, the introduction of digital learning tools was met with skepticism. Teachers and parents were concerned about the cost, the learning curve, and the potential loss of traditional teaching methods.

During a school board meeting, an advocate for digital education posed a thought-provoking question: "Imagine if every student in our district had the opportunity to learn with cutting-edge technology..."

This approach shifted the focus from the immediate challenges to the long-term benefits for students. Discussions evolved from skepticism to exploration of how digital learning could be integrated effectively. This led to the development of a phased plan that addressed concerns while progressively introducing technology into classrooms, resulting in enhanced educational outcomes and student engagement.

Case Study 3: Breaking Ground in Environmental Conservation

A non-profit organization faced considerable opposition in its efforts to establish a new conservation area. Local businesses and residents were concerned about economic impacts and restrictions on land use. The breakthrough came when the organization's leader addressed a community meeting, saying, "Imagine if this conservation effort made our region a beacon of environmental sustainability..."

This perspective encouraged the community to view the conservation project not as a limitation, but as an opportunity to lead in environmental stewardship and potentially attract eco-tourism.

By focusing on the positive possibilities, the conversation shifted from confrontation to collaboration, leading to the successful establishment of the conservation area with widespread community support.

The Mechanics of Overcoming Obstacles...

In each of these cases, "Imagine if..." functioned as a catalyst for change. It helped participants in a discussion to transcend the immediate barriers and envision a future where those barriers had been overcome. This approach does not dismiss the obstacles but rather acknowledges them as part of the journey towards a shared goal.

1. Encouraging Open-mindedness: "Imagine if..." opens up a space for creative thinking and open-mindedness. It allows individuals to step back from their entrenched positions and consider alternative viewpoints and solutions.

2. Facilitating Collaborative Problem-solving: By envisioning a positive outcome, stakeholders are more inclined to work together to overcome obstacles. It transforms a confrontational stance into a collaborative one.

3. Emotional Engagement: This phrase engages people emotionally, tapping into their hopes and aspirations. Emotional engagement is a powerful motivator in driving change and overcoming barriers.

4. Expanding the Scope of Discussion: "Imagine if..." broadens the scope of the discussion, encouraging people to think beyond the immediate and the conventional. This expanded perspective is often key in finding innovative solutions to complex problems.

The phrase "Imagine if..." is a potent tool in the art of enrolling and problem-solving. It helps in reframing obstacles as opportunities, fostering open-mindedness, collaboration, emotional engagement, and innovative thinking.

Whether in urban planning, educational reform, or environmental conservation, this approach has proven effective in transforming challenges into achievements.

By inviting others to imagine a different reality, we not only open the door to new possibilities but also empower them to be part of creating that reality. "Imagine if..." is not just about overcoming obstacles; it's about building bridges to a future where those obstacles no longer exist.

Section 4: Encouraging Creative Thinking

In a world that often clings to the status quo, fostering creative thinking is essential for progress and innovation. The phrase "Imagine if..." is a powerful catalyst in this regard, sparking imagination and inspiring out-of-the-box thinking. This section explores how this phrase can be used to encourage creative thinking, illustrated by three real-world examples.

The Role of "Imagine if..." in Sparking Creativity...

Creativity thrives on the ability to envision new possibilities and question established norms. "Imagine if..." invites people to step outside their mental constraints and explore uncharted territories of thought. It's a prompt that not only asks for new ideas but also creates a safe space for imaginative and unconventional thinking.

Case Study 1: Reinventing a Technology Product

In the competitive world of technology, staying ahead often requires radical innovation. A tech company, known for its conventional product line, was struggling to keep up with the market. During a critical brainstorming session, the CEO challenged the team: "Imagine if our product could do something no other can..."

This open-ended question unleashed a wave of creativity among the team members. Engineers, designers, and marketers alike began thinking beyond the usual feature upgrades and incremental improvements. The result was a groundbreaking product that not only captured the market's attention but also set a new standard in the industry.

Case Study 2: Transforming City Landscapes

Urban planning can often become bogged down in bureaucratic and conventional thinking. A city facing urban decay and a lack of community spaces presented a unique challenge. An innovative urban planner addressed the city council with a provocative question: "Imagine if our city's abandoned spaces were transformed into vibrant community hubs..."

This vision sparked a creative overhaul of city planning. Architects, artists, and community leaders came together to transform neglected areas into parks, community centers, and public art spaces. This creative approach not only beautified the city but also fostered a stronger sense of community and belonging among its residents.

Case Study 3: Revolutionizing Education

The field of education is often resistant to change, clinging to traditional methods and systems. A school district facing declining student engagement and achievement scores needed a new approach. A forward-thinking superintendent posed to the board, "Imagine if our classrooms were places where students are co-creators of their learning experience..."

This proposition led to a radical shift in teaching methodologies. Classrooms became centers of active learning, with teachers facilitating rather than dictating the learning process. Project-based learning, technology integration, and student-led initiatives became the norm. The result was a significant increase in student engagement, creativity, and academic achievement.

The Mechanics of Fostering Creativity...

In each of these cases, "Imagine if..." functioned as more than a question; it was a springboard into creative exploration. It encouraged participants to break free from conventional thinking and envision bold, innovative solutions.

1. Breaking Mental Barriers: The phrase challenges existing beliefs and assumptions, prompting individuals to think beyond what is to what could be.

2. Encouraging Risk-taking: By envisioning a scenario where the risk has paid off, individuals feel more comfortable proposing and embracing unconventional ideas.

3. Facilitating Diverse Perspectives: This approach brings together varied viewpoints, fostering a collaborative environment where creativity can flourish.

4. Emphasizing Possibilities Over Limitations: It shifts the focus from current limitations to future possibilities, creating a more optimistic and open mindset conducive to creativity.

"Imagine if..." is a powerful tool in driving creativity and innovation. Whether in technology, urban planning, or education, this approach has shown its effectiveness in breaking the mold and inspiring new ways of thinking and doing. It's not merely about generating novel ideas; it's about creating an environment where creativity is valued, nurtured, and put into action.

By inviting people to imagine, we open the door to a world of endless possibilities. It's in this world that creative solutions to our most pressing challenges are found. "Imagine if..." is more than just a phrase; it's a mindset, a way of approaching problems and opportunities with an open, creative, and visionary spirit.

Section 5: Practical Tips

Effective communication, especially in the context of enrolling and problem-solving, often requires more than just presenting facts and arguments. The strategic use of imaginative language, particularly the phrase "Imagine if...", can be a game-changer.

This section provides practical tips on how to effectively use this phrase, bolstered by three real-world examples.

Understanding the Power of "Imagine if..."

Before delving into specific tips, it's important to recognize the power of "Imagine if..." as a tool for opening minds, creating empathy, and fostering creative solutions. It's a phrase that can transform an ordinary conversation into an exploratory journey towards understanding and agreement.

Tip 1: Timing and Context

Importance of Timing: The impact of "Imagine if..." depends greatly on when it's used in a conversation. It's most effective when the audience is ready to think beyond the immediate and obvious.

Context Matters: The phrase should be relevant to the topic at hand and resonate with the audience's values and experiences.

Example: In a community meeting discussing the redevelopment of a local park, a council member waited until the initial arguments and concerns were expressed. Then, they introduced, "Imagine if this park could meet the needs of every generation in our community..." This timely and contextually relevant use of the phrase shifted the focus from individual concerns to a collective vision, facilitating a more productive and inclusive discussion.

Tip 2: Tone and Delivery

Engaging Tone: The tone of delivery should be inviting and open, encouraging listeners to genuinely consider the scenario being presented.

Clear and Concise: While "Imagine if..." invites creative thinking, the scenario presented should be clear and concise to avoid confusion.

Example: A teacher trying to engage students in a history lesson began with a monotone delivery of facts. Realizing the lack of engagement, they shifted their approach and said with enthusiasm, "Imagine if you were living in ancient Rome..." The change in tone and the imaginative prompt captured the students' interest and made the lesson more engaging and memorable.

Tip 3: Building Upon the Idea

Encourage Participation: After presenting the initial "Imagine if..." scenario, encourage others to build upon the idea. This fosters a sense of collaboration and investment in the solution.

Guide the Discussion: While it's important to allow creative freedom, guiding the discussion back to practical and relevant points is crucial for productive outcomes.

Example: In a business brainstorming session for a new marketing strategy, the team leader said, "Imagine if our campaign could reach every household in the city..."

After initial excitement and ideas, the leader gently steered the conversation towards actionable steps, ensuring that the imaginative exercise translated into a viable plan.

Real-World Application Examples..

1. Environmental Advocacy

In a campaign to promote recycling, an environmental group struggled to engage the local community. They used "Imagine if..." to paint a picture of a future with cleaner streets and less waste. The campaign combined this imaginative approach with practical tips on recycling, leading to a significant increase in community participation in recycling programs.

2. Healthcare Reform Debate

During a debate on healthcare reform, a policy maker used "Imagine if..." to create a scenario where healthcare was accessible and affordable for all. This empathetic approach, combined with factual data, helped bridge the gap between opposing views and fostered a more constructive dialogue on practical healthcare solutions.

3. Innovation in Technology

A tech company used "Imagine if..." in a product development meeting to inspire creativity.

The phrase helped the team think beyond current technology limitations and conceptualize innovative product features that were later integrated into successful new products.

"Imagine if..." is more than just a phrase; it's a tool for opening up new horizons in any discussion or argument. By understanding its power and applying it with timing, context, and effective delivery, it's possible to transform conversations and lead them towards creative, empathetic, and practical outcomes. Whether it's in community planning, education, business, or advocacy, these tips can help harness the full potential of imaginative thinking for positive change.

CHAPTER II

Mastering Outcomes with "Wouldn't It Be Great If..."

In this chapter, we dive into a transformative approach to enrolling communication, harnessing a simple yet powerful phrase that can reshape conversations and lead to winning outcomes.

Have you ever found yourself in a heated debate or a seemingly dead-end discussion? We've all been there, facing situations where our words seem to hit walls instead of opening doors. But what if there was a key phrase that could unlock potential in every argument, a phrase that could turn the tide in your favor while fostering a positive and collaborative environment? That phrase is, "Wouldn't it be great if..."

This chapter explores how this phrase, a beacon of optimism and potentiality, can dramatically shift the dynamics of an argument or discussion.

Whether you're negotiating a deal, resolving a personal conflict, or trying to persuade a group, "Wouldn't it be great if..." is your ally in steering conversations towards constructive and agreeable outcomes.

Explanation of the Phrase's Power...

"Wouldn't it be great if..." is more than just a string of words; it's a strategic tool in effective communication. Its power lies in its ability to reframe any conversation from confrontational to collaborative, from static to dynamic. It opens the door to imagination and allows all parties involved to envision a positive outcome. This envisioning is crucial because it moves the conversation away from focusing on problems and towards exploring solutions.

When you use this phrase, you're not just presenting an argument; you're inviting others to join you in a thought experiment about what could be possible. It's a subtle shift from asserting to imagining, but this shift can have a profound impact on how your message is received. Instead of putting others on the defensive, you're encouraging them to think creatively and openly.

In this chapter, we'll explore various scenarios where this phrase has been effectively used. From boardrooms to living rooms, "Wouldn't it be great if..." has proven to be a versatile tool in a wide range of discussions. We'll analyze these scenarios to understand how you can adapt this phrase to your own conversations.

Moreover, we'll delve into the psychological underpinnings of why this phrase works. Understanding the human inclination towards positive thinking and collaborative problem-solving will help you use "Wouldn't it be great if..." more effectively. We'll also offer practical advice on tone, timing, and follow-through to ensure that when you use this phrase, it's not just heard but felt and acted upon.

Through this chapter, keep an open mind and think about the various discussions in your life where this phrase could be a game-changer. The power of possibility is at your fingertips, and mastering the art of "Wouldn't it be great if..." could be the key to unlocking successful outcomes in both your personal and professional life.

Section 1: The Psychology Behind the Phrase

The phrase "Wouldn't it be great if..." is a linguistic gem in the realm of enrolling communication. Its effectiveness lies in its deep-rooted connection with human psychology, particularly the aspects of optimism and the creative power of language. This section will delve into how this simple phrase can significantly alter the course of a conversation, transforming potential conflict into cooperative dialogue and paving the way for positive, collaborative outcomes.

1. Tapping into Optimism:

The Power of Positive Thinking:

At its core, "Wouldn't it be great if..." is an embodiment of optimism. When we talk about optimism in psychological terms, we refer to a mindset that tends to expect favorable outcomes. This phrase naturally leads the conversation towards a positive future scenario, creating a mental image of a desirable outcome. In doing so, it aligns with the inherent human bias towards positivity – a phenomenon psychologists term the 'optimism bias.' This bias leads people to believe that they are less likely to experience negative events and more likely to experience positive ones.

The Role of Hope and Aspiration...

By framing a situation in a hopeful and aspirational context, "Wouldn't it be great if..." taps into the innate human desire for betterment and success. Hope, as a psychological construct, is not just wishful thinking; it is an active, dynamic cognitive motivational system. According to psychologist Charles R. Snyder's Hope Theory, hope comprises two main components: the perceived capability to find pathways to desired goals (pathways thinking) and the perceived motivation to use those pathways (agency thinking). By encouraging listeners to envision a positive outcome, the phrase inherently boosts their sense of agency and pathway thinking.

2. The Creative Power of Language:

Framing and Cognitive Flexibility...

Language creates our reality. The words we choose and the way we structure our sentences can profoundly influence our perception of a situation. This concept is known as 'framing.' In cognitive linguistics, framing refers to how language constrains the ways individuals perceive the world. "Wouldn't it be great if..." frames the conversation in a way that highlights potential and possibility. It fosters cognitive flexibility, encouraging listeners to think beyond the current situation and consider a range of possibilities.

Eliciting Imagination and Creativity...

The phrase also serves as a gateway to imagination. When someone hears "Wouldn't it be great if...", it naturally stimulates the creative part of the brain. It encourages the listener to think imaginatively about potential solutions and outcomes. This creative process is not just fanciful thinking; it is a critical component of problem-solving and innovation. By engaging the listener's imagination, the speaker can steer the conversation towards creative and constructive avenues.

3. Shifting from Confrontation to Collaboration:

Disarming Potential Conflict...

One of the most striking effects of the phrase "Wouldn't it be great if..." is its ability to disarm potential conflict. In confrontational situations, people are often primed for defense. They anticipate opposition and thus adopt a combative stance. However, when presented with a phrase that is inherently optimistic and imaginative, the mental gears shift. The listener is taken from a mindset of opposition to one of contemplation and possibility. This shift is subtle yet powerful. It lowers defenses and opens the door to a more amicable dialogue.

Building a Bridge to Collaboration...

The phrase is not just about avoiding conflict; it is about actively creating a collaborative space. Collaboration requires seeing the other party not as an adversary but as a partner in problem-solving. "Wouldn't it be great if..." transforms the dynamics of the conversation. It suggests a shared journey towards a mutually beneficial outcome. This collaborative mindset is crucial in negotiations, team discussions, and even personal relationships. When both parties are encouraged to envision a positive outcome, the conversation naturally becomes more cooperative.

Encouraging Empathy and Understanding...

Moreover, "Wouldn't it be great if..." can foster empathy. By inviting others to imagine a positive scenario, it implicitly asks them to step into someone else's shoes and consider their perspective. This empathetic approach is vital in resolving conflicts and building strong, understanding relationships. It moves the dialogue away from being purely transactional to being transformational, where both parties feel heard and valued.

The phrase "Wouldn't it be great if..." is a powerful tool in the art of enrolling and communication. Its effectiveness lies in its ability to tap into the optimistic nature of human psychology, leverage the creative power of language, and shift conversations from confrontation to collaboration. By understanding the psychological underpinnings of this phrase, we can harness its power to open up new possibilities, foster empathy, and build bridges in our personal and professional interactions. This phrase is more than just words; it's a mindset, a strategy, and a pathway to positive, collaborative outcomes.

Section 2: Case Studies of Successful Use:

In this section, we explore real-world scenarios where the phrase "Wouldn't it be great if..." has been effectively employed to transform conversations and yield positive outcomes. These case studies span various contexts, demonstrating the phrase's versatility and power in different settings.

Case Study 1: In Business Negotiations

Situation: A tech startup is negotiating with a potential investor. The talks have hit a stalemate over equity percentage.

Application of the Phrase: The startup CEO, sensing the impasse, shifts the conversation by saying, "Wouldn't it be great if we found a solution that aligns with your investment goals and also preserves our company's autonomy?"

Outcome: This question reframes the negotiation from a tug-of-war over numbers to a shared quest for a mutually beneficial arrangement. It prompts the investor to consider the long-term relationship and potential growth, rather than focusing solely on the immediate equity percentage. The talks resume with a more cooperative tone, leading to an agreement satisfying both parties.

Analysis: The CEO's use of "Wouldn't it be great if..." turned a confrontational situation into a collaborative problem-solving exercise. By focusing on a positive outcome, the CEO steered the conversation away from conflict and towards a creative exploration of possibilities.

Case Study 2: In Personal Relationships

Situation: A couple is arguing about spending less time together due to work commitments.

Application of the Phrase: One partner says, "Wouldn't it be great if we could find a way to balance our professional lives with our personal time so we both feel fulfilled?"

Outcome: This phrase diffuses the tension by shifting the focus from blame to a shared goal. The couple begins to discuss practical solutions, such as dedicated date nights and occasional work-free weekends, leading to a deeper understanding and a strengthened relationship.

Analysis: The use of "Wouldn't it be great if..." in this context reframed the argument from a confrontation into a collaborative dialogue. It encouraged both partners to think creatively and empathetically, transforming a dispute into an opportunity to strengthen their bond.

Case Study 3: In Public Speaking

Situation: A community leader is addressing a divisive issue in a town hall meeting.

Application of the Phrase: The speaker begins with, "Wouldn't it be great if we worked together to find a solution that benefits everyone in our community?"

Outcome: The audience, initially polarized, starts to consider the possibility of a unified approach. The meeting becomes more of a brainstorming session, with members offering various constructive suggestions, leading to a community-driven action plan.

Analysis: The phrase "Wouldn't it be great if..." set a collaborative tone for the meeting. It encouraged the audience to shift from a mindset of opposition to one of collective problem-solving, fostering a sense of community and shared purpose.

Case Study 4: In Educational Settings

Situation: A teacher is facing resistance from students on a new curriculum.

Application of the Phrase: The teacher asks, "Wouldn't it be great if we could make this curriculum exciting and relevant to your future goals?"

Outcome: Students begin to engage, suggesting ways to make the curriculum more interesting and applicable to real-world scenarios. This leads to a more interactive and enjoyable learning experience.

Analysis: By using "Wouldn't it be great if...", the teacher transformed resistance into engagement. The phrase invited students to contribute their ideas, making them active participants in their learning process.

Case Study 5: In Team Management

Situation: A project team is struggling with low morale and missed deadlines.

Application of the Phrase: The team leader says, "Wouldn't it be great if we could turn this project into a major success story for our team?"

Outcome: The team starts discussing what's been holding them back and proposes solutions to improve their workflow and communication. Morale improves as the team members feel more involved and invested in the project's success.

Analysis: The phrase helped shift the team's focus from their current problems to a shared vision of success. It fostered a sense of unity and purpose, motivating the team to collaboratively find ways to overcome their challenges.

Case Study 6: In Conflict Resolution

Situation: Two departments in a company are in conflict over resource allocation.

Application of the Phrase: A manager intervenes with, "Wouldn't it be great if we found a way to optimize our resources in a way that benefits both departments?"

Outcome: The departments begin to discuss their needs and constraints openly, leading to a new system of resource sharing that is equitable and efficient.

The manager's use of "Wouldn't it be great if..." redirected the departments' focus from competition to cooperation. It provided a platform for open communication and collaborative problem-solving.

Case Study 7: In Customer Service

Situation: A customer is upset over a product issue.

Application of the Phrase: The customer service representative says, "Wouldn't it be great if we could resolve this issue in a way that leaves you completely satisfied with our service?"

Outcome: The customer feels heard and valued. The conversation shifts from complaints to finding a satisfactory solution, resulting in a positive outcome and a loyal customer.

Analysis: The phrase helped transition the interaction from a complaint to a solution-oriented conversation. It demonstrated the company's commitment to customer satisfaction, building trust and loyalty.

These case studies demonstrate the versatility and effectiveness of "Wouldn't it be great if..." in various contexts. From resolving personal conflicts to navigating complex business negotiations, this phrase has the power to transform challenging situations into opportunities for positive change. By encouraging a shift from confrontation to collaboration, it opens up new avenues for creative problem-solving and strengthens relationships. The key to its success lies in its ability to tap into optimism, foster empathy, and encourage a cooperative approach to conflict resolution.

Section 3: Practical Application Tips

In the previous sections, we've explored the transformative power of the phrase "Wouldn't it be great if..." and examined its successful application across various scenarios. Now, let's focus on how you can effectively incorporate this phrase into your communication toolkit. This section provides practical tips to maximize the impact of this phrase in your daily interactions, whether in personal, professional, or public settings.

Tip 1: Tone and Delivery

1. Understand the Importance of Tone:

The effectiveness of "Wouldn't it be great if..." largely depends on how it's delivered. The tone of voice should convey genuine curiosity and openness. It's not just about what you say, but how you say it. A warm, friendly, and inviting tone can make a significant difference.

2. Practice Builds Mastery...:

Try practicing the phrase in front of a mirror or recording yourself to hear how you sound. Aim for a tone that is optimistic yet grounded, enthusiastic but not overbearing. Remember, your goal is to invite collaboration, not to impose your views.

Tip 2: Timing is Key

1. Choose the Right Moment:

Timing can make or break the impact of this phrase. It's most effective when introduced at a point of stalemate or rising tension. It can serve as a circuit breaker to reset the conversation's tone.

2. Avoid Overuse:

While powerful, this phrase should be used judiciously. Overuse can dilute its impact and may come off as insincere or formulaic. Use it strategically when you genuinely see an opportunity to shift the conversation towards a positive outcome.

Tip 3: Context Matters

1. Adapt to the Situation:

Tailor the phrase to suit the context of the conversation. In a professional setting, you might focus on productivity or team goals, while in personal scenarios, it might be more about feelings and relationships.

2. Be Specific:

Generalities can weaken the impact of the phrase. Be as specific as possible about the positive outcome you're envisioning. This specificity helps in painting a clearer, more compelling picture.

Tip 4: Follow-Up with Strong Arguments

1. Build on the Phrase:

After posing the question, be prepared with concrete ideas or suggestions. This shows that you're not just dreaming big but also thinking practically about how to achieve these goals.

2. Encourage Others to Contribute:

Invite others to build on the idea. This not only generates more options but also fosters a sense of shared ownership over the solution.

Tip 5: Body Language and Non-Verbal Cues

1. Reinforce with Gestures:

Your body language should reinforce the openness and collaborative nature of your message. Maintain eye contact, nod encouragingly, and use open gestures.

2. Read the Room:

Be attuned to others' non-verbal cues. If they seem receptive, continue to explore the idea. If they appear resistant, it might be worth probing their concerns before proceeding.

Tip 6: Empathy and Active Listening

1. Show Understanding:

Demonstrate empathy by acknowledging the other person's perspective before introducing the phrase. This validation can make them more receptive to your ideas.

2. Active Listening:

Listen actively to their response. This not only shows respect but also gives you valuable insights into how to steer the conversation forward.

Tip 7: Cultivating a Positive Mindset

1. Believe in the Possibility:

For "Wouldn't it be great if..." to be effective, you need to genuinely believe in the possibility you're proposing. This belief will be evident in your tone and body language.

2. Stay Open-Minded:

Be open to the ideas and suggestions that come up in response to your question. The goal is to find the best solution, which may require adapting your original idea.

Tip 8: Handling Pushback

1. Prepare for Skepticism:

Not everyone will immediately jump on board with your optimistic framing. Be prepared to handle skepticism or pushback with patience and constructive responses.

2. Reframe Resistance:

If you encounter resistance, try to reframe it as a concern that needs to be addressed in the journey towards the proposed great outcome.

Tip 9: Practice and Reflection

1. Regular Practice:

Incorporate this phrase into your daily conversations where appropriate. The more you use it, the more naturally it will come to you in critical moments.

2. Reflecting on Outcomes:

After conversations, reflect on how effectively you used the phrase and the response it elicited. This reflection will help you refine your approach.

Tip 10: Continuous Learning and Adaptation

1. Learn from Others:

Observe how others communicate and persuade. You can often pick up valuable tips and techniques to enhance your own communication style.

2. Adapt to Feedback:

Be open to feedback on your communication style. Adapt your approach based on what works best in different situations.

Mastering the use of "Wouldn't it be great if..." is about much more than just adding a new phrase to your vocabulary. It's about cultivating a mindset of optimism, collaboration, and empathy.

By paying attention to tone, timing, context, and follow-up, and by practicing active listening and empathy, you can transform this simple phrase into a powerful tool for positive change.

Remember, effective communication is a skill that requires continuous practice and adaptation. Use these tips as a guide to refine your approach and become a more enrolling and impactful communicator.

Section 4: Potential Pitfalls and How to Avoid Them

While the phrase "Wouldn't it be great if..." can be a powerful tool in enrolling communication, its effectiveness can be diminished if not used wisely. In this section, we'll explore potential pitfalls associated with the use of this phrase and provide guidance on how to avoid them, ensuring that its impact remains strong and authentic.

Pitfall 1: Overuse Leading to Dilution

The Risk of Becoming Cliché...

Repeated and indiscriminate use of "Wouldn't it be great if..." can render it ineffective. If overused, it might start to sound insincere or mechanical, losing its ability to inspire and engage others.

How to Avoidz:

1. Use Sparingly and Strategically: Reserve the phrase for moments when you genuinely see an opportunity to shift the conversation positively.

2. Vary Your Language: Mix up your language and approach to keep your communication fresh and engaging. Alternatives like "Imagine if we could..." or "How about we try..." can serve a similar purpose without sounding repetitive.

Pitfall 2: Lack of Authenticity

The Importance of Sincerity...

For "Wouldn't it be great if..." to be effective, it must stem from a place of genuine belief and sincerity. If it comes across as a mere rhetorical device devoid of real conviction, it may fail to resonate with your audience.

How to Avoid:

1. Believe in Your Proposal: Ensure that you truly believe in the ideas or solutions you're suggesting. Authenticity in your voice and demeanor naturally follows when you are sincere in your convictions.

2. Align with Values and Goals: Make sure that your use of the phrase aligns with the values and goals of your audience. This alignment increases the perceived authenticity and relevance of your message.

Pitfall 3: Misjudging the Audience or Context

The Need for Contextual Awareness...

The effectiveness of the phrase can be heavily influenced by the audience's mood, expectations, and the context of the conversation. Misjudging these can lead to the phrase falling flat or even backfiring.

How to Avoid:

1. Read the Room: Be attuned to the audience's mood and the conversation's tone. If the situation is particularly tense or the stakes are high, a direct approach may be more appropriate.

2. Cultural Sensitivity: Be aware of cultural differences in communication styles. What works in one cultural context may not be effective in another.

Pitfall 4: Unrealistic or Vague Propositions

The Trap of Wishful Thinking...

"Wouldn't it be great if..." loses its power if used to propose unrealistic or overly vague ideas. This can lead to the audience dismissing your suggestions as impractical or disconnected from reality.

How to Avoid:

1. Stay Grounded: While the phrase is meant to inspire, ensure that your propositions are still grounded in reality and achievable.

2. Be Specific: Provide enough details to paint a clear picture of what you are proposing. Vague ideas are less likely to inspire action or agreement.

Pitfall 5: Failure to Follow Through

The Expectation of Action...

Using "Wouldn't it be great if..." raises expectations of a follow-up action or discussion. Failure to follow through can lead to a loss of credibility and trust.

How to Avoid:

1. Have a Plan: Be prepared with concrete next steps or ideas to back up your proposition.

2. Commit to Action: Show commitment to exploring or implementing the ideas discussed. This builds trust and shows that you are not just ideating but are also willing to act.

Pitfall 6: Overlooking the Need for Consensus

Ignoring the Collaborative Aspect...

The phrase is meant to open up a dialogue, not to dictate a singular vision. Ignoring the collaborative aspect can lead to resistance or disengagement.

How to Avoid:

1. Invite Participation: Encourage others to contribute their thoughts and ideas. This fosters a sense of shared ownership and collaboration.

2. Value Diverse Perspectives: Be open to modifying your ideas based on input from others. This shows respect for different perspectives and enhances the likelihood of finding a mutually agreeable solution.

Pitfall 7: Mismatching Tone and Content

The Dissonance Between Tone and Message...

The tone in which "Wouldn't it be great if..." is delivered should match the content of the message. A mismatch can create confusion or skepticism.

How to Avoid:

1. Consistent Messaging: Ensure that your tone, body language, and content are in harmony. This consistency reinforces your message's authenticity and effectiveness.

2. Adapt Tone to Situation: Be mindful of the situation and adjust your tone accordingly. A serious topic may require a more subdued tone, even when framing it optimistically.

Pitfall 8: Neglecting Non-Verbal Cues

The Role of Body Language...

Non-verbal cues play a significant role in communication. Neglecting these cues can undermine the impact of your words.

How to Avoid:

1. Conscious Body Language: Use open and engaging body language to complement your message. This includes maintaining eye contact, nodding, and open hand gestures.

2. Respond to Audience Cues: Be attentive to the audience's non-verbal responses and adjust your approach if necessary. This responsiveness shows that you are engaged and attentive.

While "Wouldn't it be great if..." is a powerful tool in the art of enrolling and communication, its effectiveness hinges on thoughtful and strategic use. By being mindful of these potential pitfalls and actively working to avoid them, you can ensure that this phrase remains a potent asset in your communication repertoire. Remember, the key is to be authentic, contextually aware, and genuinely committed to fostering collaborative and positive dialogues.

Section 5: Summary & Encouragement for Practice

In this comprehensive exploration of "Wouldn't it be great if..." as a tool for resolving arguments and fostering productive conversations, we have uncovered its psychological underpinnings, witnessed its application in various contexts through case studies, learned practical tips for its effective use, and understood how to sidestep potential pitfalls. Here, we summarize the key points and encourage you to integrate this powerful phrase into your daily interactions.

Key Points Summary:

1. Leveraging Optimism and Creativity

The phrase taps into human optimism and the creative power of language, encouraging a shift in perspective from problems to possibilities.

It reframes arguments in a positive light, promoting a forward-thinking mindset and fostering a constructive approach to conflict resolution.

2. Shifting from Confrontation to Collaboration

"Wouldn't it be great if..." transforms confrontational energy into collaborative dialogue, paving the way for mutual understanding and creative problem-solving.

It disarms defensive attitudes, allowing for a more open and empathetic exchange of ideas.

3. Real-World Applications:

Case studies across various contexts, including business, personal relationships, and public speaking, have demonstrated the phrase's versatility and effectiveness.

In each scenario, it has proven to be a catalyst for turning challenging conversations into opportunities for positive outcomes.

4. Practical Application Tips:

The effectiveness of the phrase is enhanced by a sincere tone, appropriate timing, and context-specific adaptation.

Following up with strong, actionable arguments and encouraging collaborative input are crucial for maintaining the phrase's impact.

5. Avoiding Pitfalls:

Avoid overuse and remain authentic to prevent the phrase from losing its impact.

Be mindful of the audience, context, and realistic outcomes, ensuring that the phrase aligns with the situation at hand.

Encouragement for Practice:

Now that we've explored the multifaceted nature of "Wouldn't it be great if...", it's time to put this knowledge into practice. Integrating this phrase into your daily conversations can significantly enhance your communication skills and ability to resolve conflicts constructively.

1. Start Small:

Begin by using the phrase in low-stakes conversations. This could be as simple as proposing new ideas during a casual chat with friends or family.

2. Reflect and Adapt:

After using the phrase, reflect on the conversation's outcome. Did it help in steering the conversation positively? How did others react?

Use these reflections to refine your approach.

3. Expand to More Challenging Scenarios:

Gradually incorporate the phrase into more challenging conversations, such as workplace discussions or in situations where you anticipate disagreement.

4. Observe and Learn:

Pay attention to how others respond to this approach and be open to learning from these interactions. Observe if it helps in reducing conflict and fostering a more collaborative atmosphere.

5. Cultivate a Habit:

Make "Wouldn't it be great if..." a part of your communication toolkit. The more you use it, the more naturally it will come to you when needed.

6. Share Your Experiences:

As you become more comfortable with the phrase, share your experiences with others. Discussing its impact can provide valuable insights and encourage others to try it.

7. Stay Open and Flexible:

Remember, the goal is not to win every argument but to find the best possible outcome for all parties involved. Stay open to different perspectives and flexible in your approach.

8. Embrace Continuous Discovery:

Communication is an art that evolves with practice. Embrace every conversation as an opportunity to learn and grow.

"Wouldn't it be great if..." is more than just a phrase; it's a mindset that embraces optimism, collaboration, and creativity. Its power lies in its ability to transform potentially negative interactions into positive dialogues and mutually beneficial outcomes.

By practicing the strategic use of this phrase in your daily conversations, you can enhance your ability to navigate disagreements constructively and foster a more collaborative environment, whether at home, work, or in social settings.

Remember, effective communication is a journey, not a destination, and each conversation is a step forward in that journey.

CHAPTER III

Perfecting the Art of Enrollment with "I Understand Your Concerns But Consider This..."

This is a pivotal chapter in our journey through the landscape of enrolling communication. We delve into a phrase that possesses the subtle power to shift perspectives and disarm opposition: "I understand your concerns, but consider this..."

The Magic of Acknowledgement and Pivoting:

The phrase "I understand your concerns, but consider this..." works on two levels. First, it acknowledges and validates the listener's point of view, creating a foundation of respect and understanding.

Second, it smoothly pivots the conversation to present an alternative perspective or solution. This dual approach is key in transforming resistance into receptivity.

Section 1: The Psychology Behind the Phrase "I Understand Your Concerns, But Consider This..."

In the intricate dance of communication and enrollment, few phrases carry as much tact and empathy as "I understand your concerns, but consider this..." This section delves into the psychological mechanisms that make this phrase an effective tool in enrolling, supplemented by three real-world examples.

Understanding Empathy in Enrollment...

The phrase begins with an acknowledgment of the other person's concerns, which is a fundamental aspect of empathy. By demonstrating understanding, the speaker builds a bridge of trust and reduces the listener's defensiveness, creating a conducive environment for open dialogue.

Example 1: Resolving Customer Complaints

In a customer service scenario, a customer approached with a complaint about a product. The service representative replied, "I understand your concerns about the product's performance, but consider this: we have a comprehensive warranty program that can provide a free replacement or repair." This approach calmed the customer, who felt heard and valued, leading to a satisfactory resolution and maintaining customer loyalty.

The Power of Cognitive Reappraisal...

The pivot marked by "but consider this..." is a form of cognitive reappraisal. It invites the listener to reevaluate their perspective, considering new information or viewing the situation from a different angle.

Example 2: Workplace Conflict Resolution

In a workplace where two departments were in conflict over resource allocation, a manager intervened saying, "I understand your concerns about departmental budgets, but consider this: by pooling our resources, we can achieve greater efficiency and better results for both departments." This intervention helped both parties see the mutual benefits, fostering a collaborative approach to resource management.

Balancing Emotional and Rational Appeals...

The phrase masterfully balances emotional appeal (acknowledgement of concerns) with rational appeal (presenting a logical argument or alternative). This balance is crucial in enrolling them effectively without alienating the listener.

Example 3: Public Health Campaign on Healthy Eating

In a campaign aimed at addressing skepticism about adopting a plant-based diet, a public health official might encounter resistance due to misconceptions about nutritional adequacy. They might say, "I understand your concerns about a planet-based diet, but consider this: extensive research shows that plant-baed diets are highly effective if done correctly." This approach acknowledges the emotional fears around plant-baed diets while providing factual, rational information to counter misinformation.

The Role of Active Listening...

Before employing the phrase, it's imperative to engage in active listening. This ensures that the acknowledgment part of the phrase is genuine and informed, rather than a mere rhetorical tactic.

1. Reflective Listening: Mirroring back what you've heard to show that you truly understand the other person's point of view.

2. Validating Feelings: Acknowledging the emotions behind the concerns, not just the content of the concerns.

Effective Pivot to Alternative Perspectives...

The pivot marked by "but consider this..." should be smooth and feel like a natural progression of the conversation, rather than a jarring pivot.

1. Logical Flow: Ensure that the alternative perspective or solution presented is logically connected to the concerns raised.

2. Avoiding Dismissal: The pivot shouldn't feel dismissive of the concerns but rather build upon them to offer a new viewpoint.

The phrase "I understand your concerns, but consider this..." is a powerful tool in the art of enrollment, combining empathy with rational argumentation. It enables the speaker to connect emotionally, reduce defensiveness, and introduce new perspectives in a respectful and effective manner.

By understanding and applying the psychological principles behind this phrase, individuals can enhance their communication skills, leading to more productive and positive interactions in various contexts.

Whether it's in customer service, workplace collaboration, public health, or any other area, this phrase can be a key to unlocking more harmonious and constructive dialogues.

Section 2: Examples of "I Understand Your Concerns, But Consider This..."

The phrase "I understand your concerns, but consider this..." is not just a theoretical concept; it has practical applications in a myriad of real-world situations. In this section, we explore three distinct examples where this phrase has been effectively employed to navigate complex scenarios, reshape conversations, and achieve positive outcomes.

Example 1: Navigating Business Negotiations

In the high-stakes arena of business negotiations, understanding and addressing concerns while steering the conversation towards a mutually beneficial outcome is key.

Scenario: A software company, "TechFlow," is negotiating a contract with a potential client, "EcoEnterprises." The client is hesitant about the high cost of the software.

Application of the Phrase: The TechFlow representative says, "I understand your concerns about the cost of our software, but consider this: our software is designed to increase efficiency and reduce operational costs significantly. In the long term, it's an investment that will pay for itself many times over."

Outcome: By acknowledging the client's concern about the cost and then pivoting to the long-term benefits and ROI, TechFlow is able to reframe the cost from a financial burden to a valuable investment. This approach leads to a successful negotiation, with EcoEnterprises agreeing to the contract.

Example 2: Public Policy Advocacy

Effective advocacy often involves addressing public apprehensions and presenting alternative, beneficial viewpoints.

Scenario: A new public transportation project is proposed in a city, facing opposition from a segment of residents concerned about the disruption it would cause.

Application of the Phrase: A city councilor addressing a public meeting says, "I understand your concerns about the construction disruption this project will cause, but consider this: once completed, this new transportation line will reduce traffic congestion, lower pollution, and improve overall quality of life in our city."

Outcome: By first acknowledging the valid concerns about construction disruption, the councilor creates a space of empathy. Following this with a focus on the long-term benefits of the project helps residents to see the broader picture and the lasting positive impacts. This approach facilitates a shift in public opinion, with more residents supporting the project.

Example 3: Resolving Workplace Conflicts

Workplace conflicts can often escalate if not addressed with a combination of empathy and logic.

Scenario: There is a disagreement between two teams in a company, "Innovate Inc.," over the allocation of resources for new projects.

Application of the Phrase: During a team meeting, the project manager says, "I understand your concerns about having limited resources for your projects, but consider this: if we collaborate and share resources, we can combine our strengths, work on more interdepartmental projects, and enhance our overall productivity and innovation."

Outcome: The project manager's approach of acknowledging the concerns of both teams and then suggesting a collaborative approach helps in reframing the conflict. Instead of competing for resources, teams start seeing the value in collaboration, leading to a more harmonious and productive workplace.

The Mechanics of the Phrase in Practice

1. Empathy as a Starting Point:

Each example begins with a genuine acknowledgment of concerns, which helps in lowering defenses and building trust.

2. Strategic Pivot:

The Pivot to "but consider this..." is handled tactfully, ensuring that it doesn't negate the acknowledgment but builds upon it to offer a new perspective or solution.

3. Focusing on Benefits and Solutions:

The latter part of the phrase is used to shift focus to potential benefits, solutions, or alternative perspectives that may not have been considered by the audience.

4. Outcome-Oriented:

In each scenario, the phrase is employed with a clear outcome in mind – whether it's closing a business deal, garnering support for public policy, or resolving workplace conflicts.

The practical application of "I understand your concerns, but consider this..." in these examples demonstrates its effectiveness in diverse contexts. From business negotiations and public policy debates to internal workplace conflicts, this phrase proves to be an invaluable tool in the art of enrollment and conflict resolution. By acknowledging concerns and then skillfully guiding the conversation towards positive alternatives or solutions, individuals and organizations can achieve more harmonious, productive, and mutually beneficial outcomes.

Section 3: Crafting Your Approach

In the nuanced art of enrollment, the phrase "I understand your concerns, but consider this..." serves as a powerful tool. However, its effectiveness largely hinges on two critical skills: genuine listening and the artful articulation of the pivot. This section explores these two components in depth, offering guidance on how to master each skill.

Listening Skills: The Foundation of the Pivot

Listening is the cornerstone of any meaningful conversation and is particularly vital when employing a phrase like "I understand your concerns...". It's not just about hearing the words; it's about truly understanding the emotions, motivations, and perspectives behind them.

1. Active Listening:

This involves fully concentrating on what is being said, rather than just passively hearing the words. Active listening requires you to listen with all senses and give your full attention to the speaker.

2. Reflective Listening:

This means mirroring back what the other person has said and how they feel. It's a way of confirming that you have understood their concerns correctly and empathetically.

3. Avoiding Assumptions:

Making assumptions can lead to misunderstandings. Listen with an open mind and avoid jumping to conclusions before the other person has finished speaking.

4. Nonverbal Cues:

Pay attention to nonverbal signals such as body language and tone of voice, which can often convey more than words alone.

5. Validating Feelings:

Even if you disagree, acknowledging and validating the speaker's feelings can build trust and openness. It shows that you respect their viewpoint, even as you prepare to present an alternative perspective.

Example of Listening in Action

Consider a scenario where a manager is discussing a new company policy with an employee who is visibly upset. The manager actively listens, reflects back the employee's concerns, and validates their feelings. This approach not only makes the employee feel heard but also lays the groundwork for a more receptive discussion about the policy.

Articulating the Pivot: Bridging Understanding with Enrollment

Once you have demonstrated genuine understanding, the next step is to skillfully navigate the conversation towards your perspective with the phrase, "but consider this...".

1. Seamless Pivot:

The pivot should feel like a natural extension of the acknowledgment. It shouldn't negate the concerns but rather build upon them to introduce a new viewpoint.

2. Logical Connection:

Ensure that your argument or alternative perspective is logically connected to the concerns raised. It should feel like a solution or a new way of looking at the problem, not a diversion.

3. Clarity and Conciseness:

Your argument should be clear, concise, and to the point. Avoid overcomplicating the message.

4. Empathetic Persuasion:

While presenting your perspective, maintain an empathetic tone. This shows that your intention is not to win an argument but to find a common ground or a better solution.

5. Use of Evidence and Examples:

Support your argument with relevant facts, data, and examples. This strengthens your position and shows that your perspective is well-thought-out.

Example of Articulating the Pivot

In a meeting about workplace flexibility, an employee expresses concerns about the impact of remote work on team cohesion. The manager acknowledges these concerns and then pivots with, "But consider this: by employing digital collaboration tools and scheduling regular team meetings, we can maintain, if not enhance, our team dynamics in a flexible work environment."

The Mechanics of the Phrase in Practice

1. Empathy as a Starting Point:

Each example begins with a genuine acknowledgment of concerns, which helps in lowering defenses and building trust.

2. Strategic Pivot:

The Pivot to "but consider this..." is handled tactfully, ensuring that it doesn't negate the acknowledgment but builds upon it to offer a new perspective or solution.

3. Focusing on Benefits and Solutions:

The latter part of the phrase is used to shift focus to potential benefits, solutions, or alternative perspectives that may not have been considered by the audience.

4. Outcome-Oriented:

In each scenario, the phrase is employed with a clear outcome in mind – whether it's closing a business deal, garnering support for public policy, or resolving workplace conflicts.

The practical application of "I understand your concerns, but consider this..." in these examples demonstrates its effectiveness in diverse contexts. From business negotiations and public policy debates to internal workplace conflicts, this phrase proves to be an invaluable tool in the art of enrollment and conflict resolution.

By acknowledging concerns and then skillfully guiding the conversation towards positive alternatives or solutions, individuals and organizations can achieve more harmonious, productive, and mutually beneficial outcomes.

Bringing It All Together: Listening and Pivoting in Harmony

The true mastery of "I understand your concerns, but consider this..." lies in the harmonious blend of empathetic listening and strategic pivoting. It's about creating a dialogue where both parties feel heard and respected, leading to a more open and productive conversation.

1. Practice and Feedback:

Regularly practice these skills in various settings and seek feedback on your approach.

2. Mindfulness and Adaptability:

Be mindful of the situation and be prepared to adapt your approach based on the response you receive.

3. Continuous Learning:

Keep discovering and evolving your understanding of effective communication and enrollment tactics.

Crafting your approach with "I understand your concerns, but consider this..." requires a delicate balance of empathy and enrollment. By honing your listening skills and articulating the pivot effectively, you can navigate conversations with tact, respect, and effectiveness.

This approach not only helps in resolving conflicts and addressing concerns but also paves the way for more collaborative and fruitful interactions in both personal and professional contexts.

Section 4: Practice Scenarios and Tips

The mastery of using "I understand your concerns, but consider this..." effectively in conversations is an art that can be honed through practice and understanding of nuanced communication strategies. This section provides interactive scenarios and practical tips, guiding readers to adeptly incorporate this phrase into their dialogues.

Interactive Scenarios for Mental Practice

1. Scenario: Team Project Disagreement

Situation:
You are leading a team project, and there is a disagreement about the direction of the project. One team member strongly feels that the current approach is not effective.

Application:
Listen to their concerns attentively, and then respond, "I understand your concerns about our current approach, but consider this: our strategy is aligned with the latest market research, which indicates a high potential for success. How about we integrate some of your ideas to enhance our existing plan?"

Mental Exercise:
Imagine this scenario playing out. Visualize how you would listen and then pivot the conversation using the phrase.

2. Scenario: Family Dispute Over Vacation Plans

Situation:
Your family is trying to decide where to go for vacation. Your spouse is concerned about the budget for the trip you propose.

Application:
Acknowledge their concern by saying, "I understand your concerns about the budget for this vacation, but consider this: if we adjust our plan slightly, we can still have an enjoyable experience without overspending. Let's look at some cost-effective options together."

Mental Exercise:
Envision this family discussion, focusing on how you would empathetically handle the budget concerns.

3. Scenario: Customer Service Issue

Situation:
A customer is upset about a delay in service. They are expressing their dissatisfaction.

Application:
Respond with, "I understand your concerns about the delay, but consider this: we are currently upgrading our system to serve you better in the future. As a token of our apology, we would like to offer you a discount on your next purchase."

Mental Exercise:
Picture yourself in a customer service role, dealing with an upset customer. How would you use the phrase to defuse the situation and offer a solution?

Practical Tips on Tone, Body Language, and Word Choice:

1. Tone of Voice

Empathetic and Calm:

Your tone should convey empathy and understanding. A calm and composed voice helps in reducing the other person's defensiveness.

Confident but Not Confrontational:

While you need to sound confident in your perspective, avoid a confrontational tone as it can escalate the situation.

2. Body Language

Open and Receptive Posture:

Use an open body posture. Avoid crossing your arms or displaying any body language that might be perceived as defensive or closed off.

Maintain Appropriate Eye Contact:

Eye contact shows that you are engaged and sincere. However, be mindful not to stare, as it can be intimidating.

Nodding and Facial Expressions:

Nodding and appropriate facial expressions can show that you are actively listening and understanding their concerns.

3. Word Choice

Use of Empathetic Language:

Words like "understand," "hear," and "acknowledge" can reinforce your empathy.

Positive Framing:

Frame your alternative perspective positively. Focus on solutions and possibilities rather than problems.

Simple and Clear Language:

Avoid jargon or overly complex language. Your goal is to communicate clearly and effectively.

4. Practicing Active Listening

Reflect and Clarify:

Practice reflecting and clarifying what you have heard before responding. This ensures you have understood the concerns accurately.

Ask Open-Ended Questions:

This encourages the other person to express their thoughts more fully, giving you a better understanding of their perspective.

5. Handling Emotional Responses

Stay Composed:

If the conversation becomes emotionally charged, focus on maintaining your composure.

Acknowledge Emotions:

Recognize and acknowledge the emotions being expressed, but steer the conversation back to a rational and productive dialogue.

6. Building Trust

Consistency and Sincerity:

Be consistent in your empathetic approach and sincere in your responses. Trust is built when people feel heard and respected.

Mastering the use of "I understand your concerns, but consider this..." in everyday conversations is a valuable skill that enhances effective communication and problem-solving.

By practicing the provided scenarios mentally and applying the practical tips on tone, body language, and word choice, individuals can significantly improve their ability to navigate complex conversations, resolve conflicts, and build positive relationships. This phrase, when used correctly, not only helps in addressing immediate concerns but also paves the way for more open, empathetic, and constructive interactions.

Section 5: Avoiding Common Pitfalls

Mastering the phrase "I understand your concerns, but consider this..." can significantly enhance your enrolling communication. However, its effectiveness can be diminished by certain pitfalls. This section delves into key areas to watch out for, focusing on avoiding overuse of the phrase and striking the right balance between empathy and assertiveness.

Not Overusing the Phrase

The overuse of "I understand your concerns, but consider this..." can render it ineffective, making it sound insincere or formulaic.

Here's how to avoid this pitfall:

1. Variety in Language:

Use different phrases to show understanding and introduce new perspectives. Alternatives like "That's a valid point, however..." or "Your viewpoint is completely understandable, yet I'd like to add..." can convey the same meaning without repetition.

2. Sincerity is Key:

Ensure that every time you use the phrase, it is grounded in genuine understanding. If your acknowledgment of the other person's concerns doesn't feel sincere, the phrase loses its power.

3. Contextual Usage:

Reserve the phrase for situations where there is a clear need to acknowledge a concern and provide an alternative perspective. Using it as a default response in every conversation can diminish its impact.

4. Reflecting Real Understanding:

Before using the phrase, make sure you have a solid grasp of the other person's concerns. Parroting the phrase without a real understanding can come off as patronizing.

Balancing Empathy and Assertiveness

In enrolling communication, finding the equilibrium between being empathetic and assertive is crucial.

Here's how to strike that balance:

1. Empathy Doesn't Mean Agreement:

Understand that being empathetic doesn't necessarily mean you agree with the other person's point of view. It means you respect and understand where they are coming from.

2. Confidence in Your Perspective:

While being empathetic, also be confident in presenting your viewpoint. It's about respectfully offering an alternative perspective that they may not have considered.

3. Non-verbal Cues:

Your body language and tone should reflect both empathy and assertiveness. Maintain open body language and a steady, calm tone that conveys confidence without being aggressive.

4. Assertiveness with Tact:

Present your perspective firmly but tactfully. It's important to be clear and direct without being confrontational or dismissive of the other person's views.

5. Listening First, Responding Second:

Allow the other person to fully express their concerns before you respond. This demonstrates empathy and gives you a solid foundation to assert your perspective.

6. Use of "I" Statements:

Frame your perspective using "I" statements. For example, "I see it differently…" or "I have a different perspective…" This approach is less confrontational and personalizes your viewpoint.

Examples of Balancing Empathy and Assertiveness

1. In a Manager-Employee Meeting:

An employee expresses concerns about workload. The manager empathetically acknowledges this but assertively introduces a new time-management tool that could help, explaining its benefits and offering training.

2. In a Sales Situation:

A customer is hesitant about the price. The salesperson empathizes with the concern about cost but assertively explains the long-term value and cost-effectiveness of the product.

3. During a Family Discussion:

When discussing a sensitive topic like finances, one family member might express anxiety. Acknowledge their fears, then assertively present a well-thought-out budget plan that addresses these concerns.

Avoiding the overuse of "I understand your concerns, but consider this..." and striking the right balance between empathy and assertiveness are crucial for effective communication. By being mindful of these pitfalls and actively working to maintain this balance, you can use this phrase to its fullest potential, enhancing your enrolling abilities and fostering more productive and positive interactions.

CHAPTER IV

Enrolling Through the Suggestion "I'm Not Sure If This Is For You But Maybe You Know Someone..."

In this captivating chapter in our exploration of enrolling communication, focusing on the subtle yet powerful phrase, "I'm not sure if it's for you, but maybe you know someone...".

This chapter will guide you through the art of suggesting rather than insisting, a technique that can subtly shift a listener's perspective and open up new avenues for agreement and action.

The Art of Indirect Suggestion

This phrase works on the principle of indirect suggestion. It lowers the listener's resistance by not directly imposing an idea or product. Instead, it opens a backdoor into their thought process, allowing them to consider the proposition more openly and without pressure.

Section 1: Why to Use Indirect Suggestion

The Non-Threatening Approach:

The phrase "I'm not sure if it's for you, but maybe you know someone..." embodies a non-threatening approach to suggestion. Its effectiveness lies in its subtlety and the psychological comfort it provides to the listener.

1. Reducing Sales Pressure:

Traditional direct selling methods can often put listeners on the defensive, as they feel the pressure to make an immediate decision. This phrase, however, removes that immediacy and pressure. It's less about making a sale and more about sharing information, which is psychologically less demanding.

2. Space for Decision Making:

By suggesting that the listener might know someone who could benefit, it indirectly invites them to consider the proposal themselves, but without the pressure of a direct sales pitch. This space allows for a more relaxed evaluation of the information or proposal being presented.

3. The Principle of Choice:

People like to have control over their decisions. This phrase subtly gives them a choice, either to consider the proposition for themselves or to think of someone else who might be interested. This sense of control is psychologically reassuring and increases receptiveness.

Example in Action

Imagine a scenario where a financial advisor is discussing investment opportunities. Rather than directly suggesting a specific investment plan, they say, "I'm not sure if it's for you, but maybe you know someone who would be interested in diversifying their investment portfolio." This approach reduces the pressure on the potential client, making them more open to considering the proposal themselves or recommending it to someone else.

Creating Openness

Indirect suggestion, as seen in the phrase "I'm not sure if it's for you, but maybe you know someone…", creates a psychological environment that fosters openness and curiosity rather than resistance.

1. Lowering Defensive Barriers:

Direct suggestions or proposals, especially in a selling or persuasion context, can raise defensive barriers. An indirect approach lowers these barriers, as the listener doesn't feel like they are being sold to or persuaded aggressively.

2. Stimulating Curiosity:

The phrase piques interest and curiosity. When the pressure to respond is removed, the listener is more likely to genuinely consider the idea or product. It can also lead to the listener asking more questions, thereby increasing engagement.

3. The Power of Implied Endorsement:

The phrase subtly implies that the product or idea is already of interest or benefit to others. This indirect endorsement can make the listener more open to considering it.

Example in Action

Consider a health coach discussing a new wellness program. Rather than directly asking someone to join, they might say, "I'm not sure if it's for you, but maybe you know someone who's looking to improve their wellness routine." This approach might lead the listener to consider who in their circle could benefit, and in doing so, reflect on their own interest in the program.

The Role of Suggestion in Enrollment

1. Subconscious Processing:

When a suggestion is made indirectly, it often bypasses conscious resistance and is processed at a subconscious level. The listener may find themselves considering the proposal on their own terms, making them more likely to be receptive to it.

2. Creating Mental Imagery:

The phrase encourages the listener to think of others who might benefit, which inadvertently leads them to visualize the benefits, thereby creating a mental image of the product's or idea's effectiveness.

3. The Rule of Reciprocity:

By presenting the suggestion as a helpful idea for someone else, it can trigger a sense of reciprocity. The listener might feel inclined to return the favor, either by considering the proposal themselves or by referring it to someone else.

Example in Action

An educational consultant discussing a new learning method with a school administrator might say, "I'm not sure if it's for you, but maybe you know a teacher who is looking for innovative teaching methods."
This approach might lead the administrator to discuss the method with teachers, increasing its exposure and consideration.

The psychology behind the phrase "I'm not sure if it's for you, but maybe you know someone…" is grounded in its non-threatening, indirect approach which fosters openness and curiosity.

By understanding and leveraging this approach, individuals can enhance their enrolling communication, making their interactions more effective and less confrontational.

This technique, when used skillfully, opens doors to opportunities that might have been closed under the pressure of direct enrolling methods.

Section 2: Examples of the Phrase at Work

The phrase "I'm not sure if it's for you, but maybe you know someone…" has versatile applications in various real-world scenarios. This section will explore four distinct examples that illustrate the effectiveness of this subtle yet powerful approach.

Example 1: Innovative Product Launch

Context: A tech startup is launching an innovative gadget that's not yet well-known in the market.

Application: During a promotional event, the marketing head addresses the audience, "I'm not sure if it's for you, but maybe you know someone who loves trying out the latest technology. This gadget could be perfect for them."

Outcome: The audience, initially hesitant about a new product, starts thinking about friends or family who are tech enthusiasts. The phrase not only sparks interest among those who are curious about new technology but also encourages word-of-mouth promotion, effectively broadening the product's reach.

Analysis: This approach cleverly sidesteps potential resistance to a new, unfamiliar product. By shifting the focus from the audience directly purchasing to them knowing someone who might, it subtly prompts them to consider the product's features and benefits.

Example 2: Fundraising for a Non-Profit

Context: A non-profit organization is conducting a fundraising campaign for an environmental cause.

Application: The fundraiser says to a group of potential donors, "I'm not sure if this cause aligns with your current interests, but maybe you know someone passionate about environmental conservation. We would appreciate any referrals to potential supporters."

Outcome: People in the group who may not be immediately willing to donate themselves begin thinking about their network. They identify friends or colleagues passionate about environmental issues and pass on the information, leading to an increase in donations and awareness.

Analysis: This non-pressurizing approach allows individuals to feel they are contributing positively, even if they choose not to donate directly. It leverages the social networks of each individual, thus amplifying the campaign's reach.

Example 3: Real Estate Referrals

Context: A real estate agent is showcasing a new property that is outside the typical preference range of their client.

Application: During the showing, the agent remarks, "I'm not sure if this property is exactly what you're looking for, but maybe you know someone in the market for a home like this. We offer referral bonuses for any successful sale."

Outcome: The client, who might not be interested in the property for themselves, considers relatives or friends who might be looking for a property like this. The mention of a referral bonus acts as an added incentive, encouraging them to spread the word.

Analysis: This method effectively turns the client into an advocate for the real estate agent, extending the property's exposure beyond the immediate client base. It also aligns with the client's desire to help their acquaintances and benefit from the referral.

Example 4: Introducing Health and Wellness Programs

Context: A health coach is introducing a new wellness program that might not align with everyone's fitness level or interest.

Application: In a community workshop, the coach says, "I'm not sure if this program is for you, but maybe you know someone looking to start their wellness journey. We're offering a range of programs tailored to different fitness levels."

Outcome: Participants, even if they don't feel the program is right for them, start thinking about friends or family members who might benefit. This approach results in increased inquiries and sign-ups as the information is passed on to potential participants.

Analysis: By acknowledging that the program might not suit everyone and suggesting they might know someone who would benefit, the health coach removes any direct selling pressure. This makes the participants more comfortable and open to discussing and recommending the program within their circles.

In each of these examples, "I'm not sure if it's for you, but maybe you know someone…" proves to be an effective communication strategy. It works by reducing direct pressure, allowing the listener to consider the information more openly, and leveraging the power of indirect suggestion and social networks.

This phrase can be a valuable tool in various contexts, from business and non-profits to real estate and health sectors, providing a non-intrusive way to expand reach and influence.

Section 3: Crafting Your Approach

Mastering the phrase "I'm not sure if it's for you, but maybe you know someone…" involves more than just repeating these words. It requires an understanding of the listener's context and delivering the message with the right tone. This section provides insights into tailoring this phrase effectively and ensuring the delivery is engaging and genuine.

Tailoring the Suggestion:

1. Understanding the Listener

The key to effectively using this phrase lies in understanding the listener's background, interests, and needs. This requires active listening and empathy. Gather as much information as possible about the listener to make the suggestion more relevant.

2. Relating to the Listener's Interests

Once you understand the listener's interests, tailor your suggestion to align with those interests. For instance, if speaking to someone interested in technology, you might say, "I'm not sure if this latest app is for you, but maybe you know someone who loves exploring new tech."

3. Addressing the Listener's Needs

Similarly, if you are aware of a specific need or problem the listener or their acquaintance might have, tailor your suggestion to address that. For example, "I'm not sure if you're looking for financial advice, but maybe you know someone who's facing some challenges in that area."

4. Use of Anecdotes and Stories

People connect with stories more than facts. If you have anecdotes or stories that relate to the listener's context, use them alongside the phrase to make your suggestion more impactful.

5. Cultural Sensitivity

Be aware of cultural differences that might affect how your message is received. Tailoring your approach to respect these differences is crucial.

6. Avoiding Assumptions

While it's important to use what you know about the listener, avoid making broad assumptions. Keep your suggestions open-ended and flexible.

Example in Action

Imagine you're speaking to a group of young entrepreneurs about a new business tool. You know they are always looking for ways to enhance productivity. You might say, "I'm not sure if this is what your startups need right now, but maybe you know someone in your network who's struggling with productivity issues. This tool could be a game-changer for them."

Tone and Delivery:

1. Casual and Conversational Tone

The delivery of this phrase should be casual and conversational. It should feel like part of a natural dialogue rather than a rehearsed pitch. Practice saying the phrase in a way that feels like you're merely making a suggestion, not a sales pitch.

2. Authenticity

Your authenticity in delivering this phrase is crucial. If it sounds insincere or scripted, it will likely be dismissed. Speak as if you're sharing something of interest, not pushing an agenda.

3. Non-Verbal Cues

Pay attention to your body language and facial expressions. Ensure they are in sync with your words, conveying openness and sincerity.

4. Voice Modulation

Use voice modulation to emphasize certain parts of the phrase, particularly the part that relates directly to the listener's interests or needs. This helps in capturing and maintaining their attention.

5. Pacing and Pausing

The pacing of your delivery should be steady - not too fast to seem rushed, nor too slow to seem dull. Strategic pauses after the phrase can give the listener a moment to process the suggestion.

6. Flexibility in Approach

Be prepared to adapt your tone and approach based on the listener's reaction. If they seem interested, you can elaborate. If they seem indifferent, it's better not to push further.

Example in Action

Consider a scenario where you're talking to a neighbor about a community event. Your neighbor doesn't seem very interested in community gatherings. You might say, "I'm not sure if you're into these sorts of events, but maybe you know someone in the area who'd be interested. We're trying to get more people involved in community building." This non-pushy, conversational approach can pique their interest or encourage them to spread the word.

Tailoring the phrase "I'm not sure if it's for you, but maybe you know someone…" to the listener's background, interests, and needs, and delivering it in a casual, conversational tone enhances its effectiveness significantly. It's a subtle art that, when mastered, can open up new avenues for conversation, networking, and influence. The key lies in understanding the listener, being authentic, and communicating in a way that is engaging, respectful, and sincere.

Section 4: Practice Scenarios and Tips

To effectively utilize the phrase "I'm not sure if it's for you, but maybe you know someone…", it's beneficial to engage in various hypothetical scenarios. This section provides interactive scenarios across different contexts along with practical tips for observing and reacting to the listener's responses.

Interactive Scenarios:

1. Scenario: Retail Sales Setting

Situation: You're a salesperson in an electronics store. A customer seems hesitant about buying a high-end camera.

Practice Phrase: "I'm not sure if this camera is for you, but maybe you know someone who's a photography enthusiast. This model is currently the top choice for professional photography."

Goal: Encourage the customer to consider the camera either for someone they know or reevaluate it for themselves.

2. Scenario: Business-to-Business (B2B) Sales

Situation: You're pitching a new software tool to a company that seems unconvinced about its applicability to their business.

Practice Phrase: "I'm not sure if this software is for your current operations, but maybe you know a business associate who is looking to enhance their digital tools. We've seen great results in similar industries."

Goal: Broaden the conversation to include potential referrals, indirectly highlighting the software's benefits.

3. Scenario: Real Estate

Situation: You are showing a house that's above the client's stated budget.

Practice Phrase: "I'm not sure if this house is within your budget, but maybe you know someone who's looking for a property like this. We're offering an attractive commission for referrals."

Goal: Give the client a no-pressure situation to consider the house, either for themselves or for someone they know.

4. Scenario: Networking Event

Situation: You're at a networking event talking about your new business venture.

Practice Phrase: "I'm not sure if our services are what you're looking for right now, but maybe you know someone in your network who needs what we offer. We specialize in custom solutions."

Goal: Use the event as an opportunity to spread awareness about your business indirectly.

Practical Tips:

1. Observing Non-Verbal Cues

Pay close attention to the listener's body language. Are they leaning in with interest or stepping back? Adjust your approach based on these cues. For example, if they lean in, they might be interested for themselves or someone they know.

2. Listening to Verbal Feedback

Be attentive to what and how they respond. Are they asking questions or changing the subject? If they show curiosity, it's a sign to provide more details.

3. Adjusting Your Approach Based on Response

If the listener seems interested, you can elaborate. If they seem indifferent, it might be better to shift the conversation to other topics.

4. Encouraging Questions

Invite the listener to ask questions. This not only engages them but also gives you insights into their interests or concerns.

5. Follow-Up Without Pressure

If the listener shows some interest, follow up in a way that doesn't pressure them. For instance, "If you think of someone later, I'd be happy to provide more information."

6. Reflecting on the Interaction

After the conversation, reflect on what worked and what didn't. This reflection will help refine your approach in future interactions.

Example in Action

Imagine you are at a local community meeting discussing a new environmental initiative. You notice one of the attendees seems somewhat interested but hesitant. You approach them with, "I'm not sure if this initiative is something you'd be interested in participating in, but maybe you know other residents who are passionate about environmental causes. We're always looking for more community involvement."

As you say this, you notice the attendee's body language. They nod and ask a question about the initiative's goals. This is a positive sign, indicating interest either for themselves or someone they know.

You answer their question and provide additional information, making sure to maintain a conversational tone. After the meeting, you reflect on the interaction, considering how effective your approach was and how it could be improved in the future.

These practice scenarios and tips are designed to help you incorporate "I'm not sure if it's for you, but maybe you know someone…" into your daily interactions effectively.

By tailoring your approach to different contexts and being observant of the listener's reactions, you can use this phrase to expand your influence, build networks, and open up new opportunities in both your professional and personal life.

Section 5: Avoiding Common Pitfalls

The strategic use of "I'm not sure if it's for you, but maybe you know someone…" can be a powerful tool in various conversational contexts. However, like any technique, it can lose its effectiveness if misused or overused. This section explores how to avoid such pitfalls and strike a balance between directness and indirection.

Avoiding Overuse

1. Recognizing the Context

Use this phrase judiciously and only when it fits naturally into the conversation. It should not be forced or used as a one-size-fits-all solution in every interaction.

2. Diversifying Communication Strategies

Relying solely on this phrase can make your interactions predictable and insincere. Mix this approach with other communication strategies to keep your interactions fresh and engaging.

3. Judging Listener's Response

Pay attention to how people respond to this phrase. If you notice a pattern of disinterest or perfunctory responses, it might be a sign to use it less frequently.

4. Crafting Unique Conversations

Each interaction is unique, and your approach should reflect that. Customize your conversations based on the individual's interests and needs rather than using a templated phrase.

5. Building Authentic Relationships

Genuine connections are built on authenticity, not on repeated, mechanical interactions. Ensure your use of the phrase always feels genuine and not like a rehearsed line.

Balancing Directness and Indirection

1. Understanding the Value of Directness

While indirect suggestions can be effective, sometimes a direct approach is more appreciated. Knowing when to be straightforward can be just as important as knowing when to be subtle.

2. Reading the Room

Gauge the situation and the listener's preferences. Some people prefer direct communication and might find indirect suggestions evasive or confusing.

3. Blending the Approaches

Combining direct and indirect communication can be effective. For example, after using the phrase, you can follow up with a more direct question or statement based on the listener's reaction.

4. Clear Communication

Ensure that your indirect suggestion doesn't muddy the waters. The listener should not be left confused about your intentions or the message you are trying to convey.

5. Respecting Boundaries

Be mindful of the listener's boundaries. If they seem uncomfortable or disinterested, it's better to revert to a more direct and straightforward manner of speaking.

Real-World Application: Balancing Techniques

1. In Sales

A salesperson can use the phrase to introduce a product. If the customer seems uninterested, they can switch to a more direct approach, asking specifically what the customer is looking for.

2. In Networking

While networking, use the phrase to introduce your services or skills. Based on the response, you can either elaborate more directly on what you offer or move to another topic.

3. In Personal Relationships

When discussing a sensitive topic with a friend, start indirectly to gauge their comfort level. If they respond openly, you might choose to continue with a more direct approach.

Avoiding Misinterpretation

1. Clarity in Conversation

While using indirect suggestions, ensure that your message remains clear. The listener should not feel that you're implying something negative or hiding your true intentions.

2. Consistent Messaging

Your body language, tone, and words should be in harmony. Mixed signals can lead to misinterpretation and confusion.

3. Feedback Mechanism

Encourage feedback and be open to adjusting your communication style based on the responses you receive.

Continuous Improvement

1. Reflect on Interactions

After using the phrase in various contexts, take time to reflect on what worked and what didn't. Continuous self-reflection and adjustment are key to mastering this technique.

2. Seeking Constructive Criticism

Don't hesitate to ask for feedback from trusted colleagues, friends, or mentors on your communication style.

3. Learning from Others

Observe how skilled communicators use a mix of directness and indirectness in their conversations. Learn from their techniques and adapt them to your style.

Avoiding overuse and striking the right balance between directness and indirection when using "I'm not sure if it's for you, but maybe you know someone…" are crucial for maintaining its effectiveness. The goal is to make each conversation feel authentic, respectful, and tailored to the individual's preferences and the situation at hand.

By being mindful of these aspects and continuously refining your approach, you can use this phrase to enhance your communication skills and build more meaningful connections.

118

CHAPTER V

Overcoming Barriers with "What's Stopping Us From..."

In this insightful chapter, we explore the enrolling power of the phrase "What's stopping us from..." This chapter, explores how this question can effectively dismantle objections and foster a collaborative problem-solving approach in discussions and negotiations.

The Psychology Behind the Phrase

Understanding the phrase "What's stopping us from..." requires an appreciation of its underlying psychological principles. This question subtly shifts the listener's focus from reasons not to act to potential solutions and paths forward. It embodies a proactive mindset, encouraging the listener to identify and confront obstacles, often revealing that perceived barriers are less significant than initially thought.

Section 1: Identifying and Addressing Obstacles

Exploring Underlying Reasons...

The phrase "What's stopping us from..." is a powerful tool in uncovering the root causes of hesitation or resistance in various scenarios. It serves as an open invitation for participants to voice their concerns, fears, and perceived barriers. This exploration is vital for two reasons: it helps in understanding the real issues at hand and often reveals that these obstacles can be navigated or are based on misunderstandings or unfounded fears

1. Creating a Safe Space for Discussion

The phrase sets a tone of non-judgment and support, encouraging individuals to express their doubts or concerns openly. In a safe environment, people are more likely to reveal their true apprehensions.

2. Identifying Misconceptions

Often, what holds a decision or action back are misconceptions or incomplete information. By asking "What's stopping us from...", you can bring these misconceptions to light and address them with accurate information.

3. Understanding Emotional Barriers

Sometimes, the barriers are not just logical but emotional. The phrase helps in understanding these emotional hurdles, whether they are fear of change, feelings of inadequacy, or past negative experiences.

4. Highlighting Practical Concerns

It also brings out practical concerns that might be stopping progress, such as resource limitations, time constraints, or lack of support.

5. Encouraging Self-reflection

This question prompts individuals to reflect internally on their reasons for resistance, which is the first step towards addressing them.

Example in Action

In a company meeting discussing the adoption of a new project management software, some team members are hesitant. The team leader uses the phrase, "What's stopping us from adopting this new software?" Through discussion, it's revealed that the team is concerned about the learning curve and potential disruption to their current workflow. This realization leads to a focus on training and integration strategies to ease the transition.

Encouraging Joint Problem-Solving...

By framing the conversation around a mutual challenge, the phrase "What's stopping us from..." shifts the dynamic from confrontation to collaboration. It implicitly suggests that the problem is shared and, therefore, so should be the solution.

1. Promoting Teamwork

The phrase sets a collaborative tone for the discussion. It implies that any obstacles will be addressed collectively, fostering a sense of teamwork.

2. Shifting from Blame to Solutions

This approach prevents the blame game. Instead of pointing fingers for the lack of progress, it encourages a focus on finding solutions.

3. Breaking Down Complex Issues

Sometimes, the challenge seems insurmountable because it is viewed as one massive problem. Discussing what is stopping progress can help break down the issue into smaller, manageable parts.

4. Leveraging Diverse Perspectives

In a group setting, this question invites diverse perspectives. Different viewpoints can lead to creative and comprehensive solutions.

5. Building a Constructive Dialogue

It transforms the dialogue from arguing over differing opinions to a constructive conversation about overcoming mutual challenges.

Example in Action

Consider a community initiative to set up a local library, which is meeting resistance. A community leader asks, "What's stopping us from establishing this library?" The discussion reveals concerns about funding and location.

This leads to a brainstorming session where various members contribute ideas for fundraising and suitable locations, turning individual apprehension into collective problem-solving.

Using "What's stopping us from…" is an effective way to identify and address obstacles in any scenario. It allows for the exploration of underlying reasons behind resistance and transforms the conversation into a joint problem-solving exercise. This approach is not about dismissing concerns but about understanding and addressing them in a collective, constructive manner.

Whether in a professional setting, community project, or personal relationships, this phrase can unlock discussions, dispel fears, and pave the way for positive action and decision-making.

Section 2: Real-Word Examples

The phrase "What's stopping us from…" is a versatile tool that can be applied in numerous real-world situations to encourage proactive problem-solving and collaboration. Here are four detailed examples demonstrating its efficacy in different contexts.

Example 1: Corporate Strategy Meeting

Scenario: In a corporate setting, a company is hesitant to expand its market due to perceived risks and uncertainties.

Application: During a strategic meeting, one of the senior managers poses the question, "What's stopping us from expanding into the new market?" The discussion that follows uncovers various concerns, such as lack of market research, fear of overextension, and inadequate knowledge of the new market demographics.

Outcome: This leads to the formation of a dedicated team to conduct thorough market analysis and research. By identifying specific concerns, the company is able to address each one methodically, eventually leading to a successful market expansion.

Analysis: The phrase helped transform a vague sense of apprehension into actionable items. It turned a standstill into a strategic action plan, allowing the company to move forward with confidence.

Example 2: Environmental Community Project

Scenario: A community is grappling with whether to initiate a local recycling program due to doubts about participation levels and funding.

Application: At a community meeting, an advocate for the program asks, "What's stopping us from starting a community-wide recycling program?" This opens up a dialogue where residents express concerns about implementation, costs, and whether there would be enough community involvement.

Outcome: The conversation leads to the idea of starting a small pilot program to gauge community interest and participation. Additionally, local businesses are approached for sponsorship to cover initial costs. The pilot program's success leads to a full-scale implementation.

Analysis: The question allowed the community to move from a state of indecision to one of collective action. It also fostered community engagement and ownership of the project.

Example 3: Educational Curriculum Development

Scenario: An educational institution is considering integrating more technology into its curriculum but is hesitant due to budget constraints and teacher training.

Application: During a curriculum development meeting, a progressive educator asks, "What's stopping us from integrating more technology into our curriculum?" Through discussion, it's revealed that the main barriers are budget limitations for technology upgrades and a lack of teacher training in new technologies.

Outcome: The institution decides to seek grants for technological development and partners with tech companies for teacher training workshops. This gradual integration enhances the learning experience and keeps the institution competitive and up-to-date.

Analysis: The phrase helped in pinpointing the exact hurdles and pushed the institution to find creative solutions, ensuring that the educational needs of the students are met without compromising on the quality of education.

Example 4: Health and Fitness Personal Goal

Scenario: A person is struggling to commit to a healthier lifestyle and fitness regime.

Application: During a discussion with a fitness coach, the coach asks, "What's stopping us from committing to a fitness plan?" This leads to the realization that time management and lack of motivation are the primary hurdles.

Outcome: Together, they devise a flexible fitness schedule that fits into the individual's lifestyle. The coach also suggests a fitness accountability group to help with motivation. This personalized approach results in a consistent and enjoyable fitness routine.

Analysis: The phrase encouraged a personal reflection on barriers to a healthier lifestyle. The joint problem-solving approach between the coach and the individual led to practical and sustainable solutions.

In each of these scenarios, "What's stopping us from..." acts as a catalyst for change. It encourages individuals and groups to confront their barriers head-on, fostering an environment of open dialogue, shared problem-solving, and ultimately, progress and innovation.

Whether in corporate strategy, community projects, education, or personal goals, this phrase proves to be a valuable asset in transforming challenges into actionable plans.

Example in Action:

In a company meeting discussing remote working policies, the manager notices a divide in opinions. Some employees are enthusiastic, while others are concerned about collaboration and team dynamics.

The manager uses the phrase, "What's stopping us from finding a middle ground that addresses these concerns?" This opens up a constructive discussion where employees feel comfortable voicing their opinions, leading to a hybrid policy that meets various needs.

Crafting your approach with "What's stopping us from…" requires an understanding of the context and audience, coupled with the ability to facilitate open and constructive dialogue.

It's about creating a safe space for discussion, where the focus is on collaborative problem-solving. By tailoring the phrase to the specific situation and encouraging open dialogue, this approach can effectively lead to uncovering and overcoming barriers, fostering an environment of collective progress and solution-finding.

Section 3: Crafting Your Approach

Understanding Context and Audience...

The effectiveness of the phrase "What's stopping us from…" largely depends on how well it is tailored to the specific context and audience. Understanding the nuances of the situation and the perspectives of those involved is crucial for this approach to yield positive results.

1. Active Listening

This is the first and most important step. Listen attentively to what the audience is saying, and equally importantly, to what they are not saying. This will give you insights into their concerns, fears, and motivations.

2. Assessing the Context

Every situation is unique. A strategy meeting in a corporate setting will be different from a discussion in a community project. Understand the dynamics at play - the power structures, the emotional undertones, and the stakes involved.

3. Recognizing Individual Concerns

In any group, individuals will have their own unique viewpoints and concerns. Identify these various perspectives to tailor your approach in a way that resonates with each participant.

4. Background Research

In some cases, like a business meeting or a public forum, doing your homework beforehand can provide valuable context. Knowing the history, the data, or past attempts at solving the issue can guide your approach.

5. Adapting to Cultural Sensitivities

Be mindful of cultural nuances and sensitivities. What works in one cultural context may not be appropriate in another.

Example in Action

Imagine a scenario where a non-profit organization is considering launching a new program in a community. Before the meeting, the leader does thorough research on the community's past initiatives, cultural values, and demographic data. During the discussion, they actively listen to the concerns of the community members. Armed with this understanding, they ask, "What's stopping us from implementing this program in a way that aligns with our community values?"

Encouraging Open Dialogue...

Using "What's stopping us from..." should be more than just a tactic; it should be a genuine invitation for open, honest dialogue. It's about creating an environment where everyone feels comfortable sharing their thoughts and concerns.

1. Setting the Tone

Begin conversations with a tone of inclusivity and openness. Make it clear that all viewpoints are welcome and that the goal is to work together to find a solution.

2. Facilitating, Not Dominating

This phrase is most effective when used to facilitate discussion, not to dominate it. Encourage others to speak and share their thoughts.

3. Acknowledging and Valuing Contributions

When someone shares a concern or viewpoint, acknowledge it and show appreciation for their input. This encourages others to contribute as well.

4. Maintaining Neutrality

Especially in a leadership or facilitative role, it's important to remain neutral and not dismiss or favor particular viewpoints prematurely.

5. Guiding the Discussion Constructively

If the conversation goes off track, gently steer it back to the topic at hand. Keep the focus on identifying and overcoming barriers.

Section 4: Practice Scenarios and Tips

Interactive Scenarios:

1. Family Decision-Making

Situation: A family is debating whether to move to a new city. Some members are excited about the opportunity, while others are apprehensive.

Application: During a family meeting, someone might say, "What's stopping us from making this move? Let's lay out all our concerns." This opens the floor for each member to voice their fears and hopes, ranging from job opportunities to leaving friends behind.

Mental Practice: Imagine yourself in this family meeting. Consider the different concerns you might hear and how you would address them using "What's stopping us from…"

2. Workplace Conflict

Situation: In a project team, there's a conflict about which marketing strategy to pursue.

Application: The team leader asks, "What's stopping us from combining elements of both strategies?" This prompts team members to discuss the merits and drawbacks of each approach and explore a blended strategy.

Mental Practice: Visualize a meeting where opinions are divided. Think about how merging ideas could alleviate concerns and lead to an innovative solution.

3. Social Initiatives

Situation: A community group is hesitant to start a recycling initiative due to doubts about participation and effectiveness.

Application: A group member might say, "What's stopping us from starting small and growing our recycling initiative gradually?" This can lead to a discussion about manageable first steps and addressing concerns incrementally.

Mental Practice: Picture yourself with your community group discussing this initiative. How would you use the phrase to alleviate fears and motivate action?

4. Educational Reform

Situation: A school is considering integrating more technology in the classroom but is concerned about costs and training.

Application: During a staff meeting, a teacher could ask, "What's stopping us from seeking external funding or partnerships for our tech integration?" This could spark conversation about creative financing and support strategies.

Mental Practice: As a teacher in this scenario, think about the potential objections and how this phrase might help navigate towards solutions.

Practical Tips:

1. Tone of Voice

Collaborative Tone: Use a tone that conveys collaboration and openness. Your voice should invite discussion, not shut it down.

Avoid Aggression: Even if you are passionate about the topic, ensure your tone doesn't come across as aggressive or confrontational.

2. Body Language

Open Gestures: Use open gestures, like palms up, to signal that you are open to ideas and discussion.

Eye Contact: Maintain appropriate eye contact to show engagement and sincerity.

Nodding: Nod to show you are actively listening and considering what others are saying.

3. Timing

Right Moment: Choose the right moment to use this phrase. It's most effective when the group has hit a stalemate or is going in circles.

Pause After Asking: After posing the question, give people time to think and respond. Don't rush to fill the silence.

4. Responding to Feedback

Acknowledging Responses: Acknowledge each response to show that you value the input. Even if you disagree, acknowledge first before offering a counterpoint.

Building on Ideas: Use the feedback to build towards a solution. Show how different ideas can fit together.

5. Maintaining a Non-confrontational Stance

Neutral Wording: Choose your words carefully to maintain neutrality. Avoid language that might imply blame or judgment.

Facilitating, Not Leading: Your role is to facilitate the discussion, not to push your agenda. Let the group steer the conversation.

Example in Action

In a team meeting at work, there's a discussion about switching to a new software system. There's resistance due to the anticipated learning curve. You use the phrase, "What's stopping us from making the switch?" and follow it up with active listening, acknowledging concerns, and guiding the team to think about how the transition can be managed smoothly.

Using "What's stopping us from…" effectively requires understanding the right context and audience, delivering it with the appropriate tone and body language, and timing it perfectly. These interactive scenarios and practical tips provide a guide to practicing and refining the use of this powerful phrase across various situations.

Remember, the goal is to foster open dialogue, encourage collaborative problem-solving, and create a space where all viewpoints are considered and respected.

Section 5: Avoiding Common Pitfalls

In using the phrase "What's stopping us from…," it's crucial to navigate carefully to avoid common pitfalls that could undermine its effectiveness. This section delves into how to avoid leading questions and balance optimism with realism.

Avoiding Leading Questions:

1. Genuine Inquiry

The essence of the phrase should be rooted in genuine curiosity. It's not about leading the audience to a preconceived conclusion, but about understanding their perspectives and concerns.

2. Open-Ended Approach

Frame the question in a way that allows for a range of responses. Avoid wording that narrows down the answers to what you expect or want to hear.

3. Encouraging Diverse Opinions

Make it clear through your tone and follow-up questions that all opinions and perspectives are valued. This encourages honest and diverse responses.

4. Avoiding Assumptions

Do not embed any assumptions within your question. Assumptions can make the question seem leading and can hinder open communication.

5. Active Listening

Demonstrate through active listening that you are genuinely interested in understanding the barriers, not just in hearing your own opinions echoed back.

Example in Action

In a team discussion about delaying a project deadline, instead of saying, "What's stopping us from sticking to the original deadline?" (which implies a preference for not delaying), you could ask, "What are the key challenges we are facing with the current deadline?" This opens up a discussion about the real issues impacting the project timeline.

Balancing Optimism and Realism:

1. Acknowledging Real Challenges

While "What's stopping us from…" is an inherently optimistic phrase, it should not overlook or downplay real challenges. Recognize and validate the difficulties and obstacles brought up in the discussion.

2. Realistic Solutions

When discussing potential solutions to the identified barriers, ensure they are realistic and feasible. Overly optimistic solutions that don't consider practical limitations can lead to frustration and loss of credibility.

3. Combining Positivity with Practicality

Strive for a balance between a positive outlook and practical considerations. This helps in maintaining morale while keeping expectations grounded.

4. Setting Achievable Goals

Use the insights gained from the discussion to set goals that are challenging yet achievable. Unrealistic goals can lead to disappointment and a sense of failure.

5. Risk Assessment

Part of being realistic is assessing potential risks and having contingency plans. Discuss not only how to overcome the barriers but also what to do if things don't go as planned.

Example in Action

In a meeting about adopting a new business strategy, the phrase is used to explore why the company hasn't taken this direction before. While the team is optimistic about the new strategy, they also realistically assess the risks and potential downsides, leading to a more grounded and comprehensive plan.

In utilizing "What's stopping us from…," it's essential to ensure it comes across as a genuine inquiry and not a leading question. Additionally, balancing optimism with a realistic assessment of challenges is key to finding viable solutions.

This approach fosters an environment of open and honest communication where realistic and practical solutions can be developed collaboratively. By avoiding these pitfalls, you can effectively use this phrase to encourage productive discussions and problem-solving in various contexts.

CHAPTER VI

Guiding Perspectives "How Open-Minded Would You Be..."

This chapter explores the enrolling influence of the phrase "How open-minded would you be..." when engaged with someone in an argument or discussion, guiding them gently towards your point of view. This phrase can effectively navigate conversations, subtly influencing the listener's openness to new ideas.

The Psychology of Open-Mindedness:

At its core, "How open-minded would you be..." leverages the listener's desire to be perceived as open-minded and reasonable. This phrase taps into their subconscious willingness to consider alternative viewpoints, making them more receptive to what you are about to propose.

1. Establishing a Positive Frame

The question sets a positive frame for the conversation. It implies that being open-minded is a valued trait and that you expect the listener to possess it.

2. Subconscious Suggestion

By suggesting open-mindedness, the listener is subconsciously guided to live up to that expectation, making them more amenable to your perspective.

3. Creating a Safe Space for Discussion

The phrase invites the listener to explore new ideas without committing to them, reducing defensive barriers.

Section 1: Utilizing the Phrase in Various Contexts

In Business Negotiations...

1. Shifting the Negotiation Framework

In business negotiations, it's common for parties to enter with firm stances, often leading to adversarial interactions. Introducing the phrase, "How open-minded would you be to exploring a partnership that could mutually benefit our companies?" transforms the tone of the negotiation. It shifts from confrontational to cooperative, opening a pathway to explore mutually beneficial outcomes.

2. Creating a Win-Win Scenario

This phrase helps in redirecting the focus from individual gains to shared benefits. It encourages both parties to think beyond their immediate goals and consider long-term partnerships that could be more lucrative.

3. Encouraging Creative Thinking

By asking about open-mindedness, you invite the other party to think creatively and be more receptive to innovative ideas or unconventional proposals that they might have dismissed outright in a more adversarial setting.

4. Building Relationships

This approach fosters a sense of camaraderie and trust. Business is not just about transactions; it's also about building relationships. Showing that you value a collaborative approach can lay the groundwork for a strong and enduring business relationship.

In Personal Relationships...

1. Fostering Open Communication

Personal relationships thrive on open and honest communication. Asking, "How open-minded would you be to discussing how we can manage our finances more effectively?" initiates a conversation that might otherwise be fraught with sensitivity or defensiveness.

2. Joint Problem-Solving

This phrase sets the stage for joint problem-solving. It implies that managing finances is a shared responsibility and that both partners have an equal say in finding solutions.

3. Reducing Conflict

Money matters can be a significant source of conflict in relationships. By framing the discussion in terms of open-mindedness, you reduce the likelihood of conflict and increase the chances of reaching a mutually satisfactory agreement.

4. Enhancing Understanding and Empathy

This approach can lead to a deeper understanding of each other's perspectives and concerns about finances. It's not just about finding a practical solution; it's also about strengthening the emotional bond by showing empathy and understanding.

In Community and Social Issues...

1. Engaging the Community

In dealing with community and social issues, engagement and buy-in from the community members are crucial. "How open-minded would you be to considering some innovative solutions to our neighborhood's challenges?" is an invitation for community members to be part of the solution.

2. Valuing Community Input

This phrase shows that you value the opinions and ideas of the community members. It's not about imposing solutions but about finding them collaboratively.

3. Encouraging Diverse Perspectives

Community issues are complex and can benefit from diverse perspectives. By asking for open-mindedness, you encourage people from different backgrounds and experiences to share their ideas, leading to more comprehensive and inclusive solutions.

4. Building Community Cohesion

Working together on solutions can strengthen community bonds. When people feel that their voices are heard and that they have a stake in the outcome, it builds a sense of unity and collective purpose.

In each of these contexts, "How open-minded would you be..." serves as a powerful tool to transform conversations and negotiations. Whether in business, personal relationships, or community issues, it opens up possibilities for collaborative problem-solving and mutual understanding.

This phrase is not just about achieving immediate goals; it's about building relationships, fostering trust, and creating environments where open and constructive dialogues can flourish.

Section 2: Techniques for Effective Delivery

Mastering the art of using "How open-minded would you be…" in conversations involves more than just the words. It's about how you deliver them. This section explores various techniques that enhance the effectiveness of this phrase in different communication scenarios.

Tone and Body Language…

1. Tone of Inquiry

Use a tone that genuinely sounds inquisitive, not rhetorical. It should convey your interest in their thoughts and openness to their responses.

2. Non-Confrontational Body Language

Adopt open and relaxed body language. Avoid crossing arms or other closed-off postures. Nodding slightly while asking the question can encourage the listener to open up.

3. Maintaining Eye Contact

Eye contact conveys sincerity and engagement. It shows that you are genuinely interested in what the other person has to say.

4. Mirroring

Subtly mirror the body language of your conversation partner to create a sense of rapport and understanding.

Timing and Context…

1. Choosing the Right Moment

Timing is critical. Pose the question after you've laid some groundwork or when you sense hesitation in the conversation.

2. Contextual Relevance

Ensure that the phrase fits naturally within the context of the conversation. It should not feel out of place or forced.

3. Responding to Cues

Be attentive to verbal and non-verbal cues from your conversation partner. These cues can guide you on when to introduce the phrase effectively.

Building Rapport…

1. Establishing Trust

Building rapport and trust with the listener makes them more receptive to your questions. Engage in small talk or shared experiences before jumping into more serious topics.

2. Showing Genuine Interest

Express genuine interest in the listener's opinions and thoughts. This makes them feel valued and more open to sharing their views.

3. Acknowledging Their Perspective

Before posing the question, acknowledge what they have already shared. This shows that you are considering their viewpoint seriously.

Clarity and Conciseness...

1. Being Clear and Direct

While the phrase is open-ended, your speech should be clear and direct. Avoid using complex language or jargon that might confuse the listener.

2. Conciseness

Keep your question concise. Long-winded questions can lose the listener's interest or obscure the main point.

Follow-Up and Engagement...

1. Encouraging Elaboration

After asking the question, if the response is brief or unclear, gently encourage further elaboration. You might say, "Can you tell me more about your thoughts on this?"

2. Active Listening

Show that you are actively listening to their response. This involves nodding, maintaining eye contact, and providing verbal acknowledgments like "I see" or "That's interesting."

Managing Responses…

1. Handling Diverse Opinions

Be prepared to handle a range of responses, some of which might be contrary to your expectations. Maintain an open mind and a respectful demeanor.

2. Navigating Resistance

If you encounter resistance or a negative response, don't push. Acknowledge their stance and perhaps revisit the topic later in the conversation.

3. Staying Neutral

Maintain a neutral stance. The goal is to explore their openness, not to argue or convince them on the spot.

Using Empathy…

1. Empathetic Responses

Show empathy in your responses, especially if the topic is sensitive. This helps in maintaining a comfortable and safe space for open dialogue.

2. Understanding Emotions

Be mindful of the emotional undercurrents in the conversation. The way a person feels about the topic will influence their openness to discuss it.

Adapting to Feedback…

1. Learning from Interaction

Use each conversation as a learning experience. Reflect on what worked and what didn't, and adapt your approach accordingly.

2. Seeking Feedback

In some cases, it may be appropriate to ask for feedback on your approach, especially in ongoing relationships like with colleagues or family members.

The phrase "How open-minded would you be…" is a necessary tool in eliciting openness and collaboration in discussions, but its success heavily relies on the delivery. By paying attention to tone, body language, timing, and the context, and by building rapport and empathetically engaging with responses, you can maximize the effectiveness of this approach.

Remember, the goal is to foster open-mindedness and mutual understanding, not to win an argument or force a viewpoint.

Section 3: Enhancing Enrollment…

In enrolling communication, especially when using the phrase "How open-minded would you be…", it's essential to enhance the persuasiveness of your approach. This section explores various strategies to strengthen your enrollment skills, ensuring that your use of this phrase yields positive results.

Linking to Shared Values...

1. Identifying Common Ground

Start by identifying values, goals, or interests that you share with your audience. This forms a foundation of mutual understanding and respect.

2. Tailoring Your Message

Frame your message in a way that aligns with these shared values. This creates a sense of unity and increases the likelihood of your audience being receptive to your perspective.

For Example

In a workplace, if teamwork is a shared value, you might say, "How open-minded would you be to a new project management approach that could enhance our team's efficiency and collaboration?"

Providing Evidence and Examples...

1. Use of Data and Facts

Support your argument with relevant data, research, and facts. This adds weight to your proposal and shows that it's not just an opinion.

2. Real-World Examples

Share examples or case studies where similar ideas or approaches have been successful. This demonstrates the practicality and effectiveness of your proposal.

3. Personal Experiences

If applicable, share your own experiences. Personal stories can be powerful in making your argument relatable and convincing.

Inviting Exploration...

1. Encouraging Curiosity

Frame your argument as an invitation to explore new ideas or solutions. This approach is less aggressive than hard selling and can pique the interest of your audience.

2. Open-Ended Questions

Along with "How open-minded would you be...", use other open-ended questions to further encourage exploration and discussion.

Balancing Emotional Appeal with Logic...

1. Appealing to Emotions

While logic is important, don't underestimate the power of emotional appeal. People are often driven by emotions, so it's important to connect on an emotional level.

2. Striking the Right Balance

Too much emotion can undermine the logical aspect of your argument, and vice versa. Find a balance between appealing to emotions and presenting logical reasoning.

Anticipating and Addressing Counterarguments...

1. Preparation

Anticipate potential counterarguments or objections to your proposal. This shows that you have thought through various aspects of your idea.

2. Addressing Concerns Proactively

Proactively address these counterarguments in your discussion. This not only strengthens your argument but also shows that you are open-minded and considerate of different viewpoints.

Creating a Sense of Urgency...

1. Highlighting Timeliness

If applicable, highlight why your proposal is timely or urgent. A sense of urgency can motivate your audience to be more open-minded and consider your ideas more seriously.

2. Avoiding False Urgency

Be genuine in your portrayal of urgency. Creating a false sense of urgency can backfire and damage your credibility.

Building Credibility...

1. Demonstrating Expertise

Show that you have a deep understanding of the topic. Your expertise can significantly enhance the persuasiveness of your argument.

2. Consistency in Communication

Be consistent in your communication and follow through on your commitments. Consistency builds trust and credibility over time.

Using Enrolling Language...

1. Choice of Words

Use words that are powerful and positive. Language has a significant impact on how your message is received.

2. Avoiding Jargon

While it's important to demonstrate expertise, avoid using jargon that might confuse or alienate your audience.

Listening and Adapting…

1. Active Listening

Show that you are actively listening to your audience's responses. This demonstrates respect for their opinions and can provide insights into how to adapt your approach.

2. Flexibility

Be flexible in your approach. If you sense resistance, be willing to adjust your argument or explore different aspects of your proposal.

Enhancing enrollment when using "How open-minded would you be…" involves a combination of strategies, from linking to shared values and providing evidence, to balancing emotional and logical appeals, and building credibility.

By honing these skills, you can effectively enroll and engage your audience in open-minded discussions, leading to more fruitful and collaborative outcomes.

Remember, the key to enrollment is not just in what you say, but how you say it and how well you connect with your audience.

Section 4: Practice Scenarios and Exercises...

Practicing the use of "How open-minded would you be..." in various scenarios is crucial for mastering its application. This section provides interactive scenarios and exercises designed to help you effectively incorporate this phrase into your communication repertoire.

Scenario 1: Workplace Innovation...

Situation:

You're proposing a new digital project management tool at your workplace, but your team is accustomed to the current system and seems resistant to change.

Exercise...

Role-play:

Practice with a colleague or in front of a mirror. Present your proposal and then use the phrase, "How open-minded would you be to trying out this new project management tool for a month?"

Reflection:

After the role-play, reflect on your tone, body language, and the responses received. Consider how effectively you addressed concerns and whether you demonstrated the benefits of the new tool.

Scenario 2: Family Decision Making...

Situation:

You want to suggest a family vacation to a destination that's unconventional compared to your usual choices.

Exercise...

Discussion Simulation:

Simulate a family discussion. Introduce the idea and gauge the reaction. Then say, "How open-minded would you be to visiting [destination] for our next vacation?"

Feedback Analysis:

Analyze the simulated reactions of family members. Did the phrase encourage a more positive discussion? How could you adapt your approach based on their reactions?

Scenario 3: Educational Settings...

Situation:

As a teacher, you want to introduce a new teaching method that's different from the traditional approach.

Exercise...

Mock Presentation:

Present the new method to a group of fellow teachers or friends acting as teachers. After outlining the method, ask, "How open-minded would you be to experimenting with this new teaching approach in your classrooms?"

Observation and Adaptation:

Observe their responses and be prepared to answer questions or concerns. Reflect on how you can adapt your method based on their feedback.

Scenario 4: Health and Lifestyle Change...

Situation:

You're a fitness coach and want to suggest a new dietary plan to a client who is skeptical about changing their eating habits.

Exercise...

Client Consultation Role-play:

Conduct a mock consultation, suggesting the new dietary plan. Use the phrase, "How open-minded would you be to trying this new dietary plan for two weeks?"

Response Evaluation:

Evaluate the mock client's response to gauge how convincing your approach was. Reflect on how you can modify your presentation to make it more compelling.

Tips for Effective Practice...

1. Diverse Scenarios

Practice in a variety of scenarios to adapt to different audiences and situations.

2. Tone and Delivery

Pay attention to your tone - it should be inquisitive and open. Ensure your body language is inviting and not confrontational.

3. Active Listening

Practice active listening in your responses. Show that you are genuinely interested in what the other person has to say.

4. Adapting to Feedback

Learn to adapt your approach based on the feedback or responses you receive during these exercises.

5. Self-Reflection

After each practice session, take time to reflect on what worked well and what areas need improvement. Consider how your choice of words, tone, and body language affected the outcome.

6. Seeking External Feedback

If possible, get feedback from those you practice with. Sometimes external perspectives can provide valuable insights into your communication style.

Incorporating Feedback...

1. Feedback Integration

Use the feedback to refine your approach. If someone suggests that your tone seemed insincere, practice being more genuine.

2. Understanding Different Perspectives

Recognize that different people may react differently to the same approach. Use this understanding to tailor your communication to individual preferences and styles.

3. Continuous Improvement

View each exercise as an opportunity for growth. The goal is to continually improve your ability to persuade and influence through open-minded discussions.

Practicing "How open-minded would you be…" in various scenarios enhances your ability to use this phrase effectively in real-life situations.

By engaging in these exercises and incorporating feedback, you can develop a persuasive communication style that is both influential and respectful of others' viewpoints.

Remember, the most effective communication is adaptive, empathetic, and considerate of the audience's perspectives.

Section 5: Navigating Challenges and Objections…

Navigating challenges and objections is a critical aspect of enrolling communication, especially when using a phrase like "How open-minded would you be…". This section is dedicated to strategies for handling objections and challenges effectively, ensuring a constructive and positive dialogue.

1. Understanding the Nature of Objections...

Root Cause Analysis:

Often, objections are not what they seem on the surface. It's essential to understand the underlying reasons behind objections, whether they stem from fear, misunderstanding, lack of information, or past experiences.

Empathetic Listening:

Listen empathetically to objections. This not only shows respect for the other person's viewpoint but also provides valuable insight into their perspective.

Separating Person from Problem:

When navigating objections, focus on the issue at hand rather than making it about the person. This helps maintain a positive and productive conversation.

2. Responding to Objections...

Acknowledging Concerns:

Start by acknowledging the objection. This shows that you are taking the other person's concerns seriously and are not dismissive.

Clarifying Questions:

Ask clarifying questions to fully understand the objection. This can also encourage the other person to think more deeply about their concerns.

Reframing the Objection:

Try to reframe the objection in a way that aligns with your argument. For example, if the concern is about the cost, highlight the long-term savings or value.

3. Overcoming Common Challenges...

Resistance to Change:

Resistance is often due to fear of the unknown. Address this by providing clear, factual information and examples of successful implementation.

Misinformation:

If the objection is based on misinformation, gently correct it with accurate data and sources. Be careful not to come across as condescending.

Lack of Interest:

Spark interest by connecting the topic to something the person cares about. Show how your proposal can benefit them personally or professionally.

4. Techniques for Maintaining a Positive Dialogue...

Stay Calm and Composed:

Keep your emotions in check. Getting defensive or aggressive can derail the conversation.

Use of Positive Language:

Use positive language that focuses on solutions rather than problems. Avoid negative phrasing that could escalate tensions.

Encouraging Participation:

Make the conversation collaborative. Encourage the other person to suggest alternatives or improvements to your proposal.

5. Handling Complex Objections...

Breaking Down Complex Issues:

If an objection is complex, break it down into smaller, more manageable parts. Address each part separately.

Seeking Common Ground:

Find areas of agreement that you can build on. This can create a foundation for resolving more contentious issues.

Expert Opinions and Case Studies:

In some cases, bringing in expert opinions or relevant case studies can help in addressing complex objections.

6. Adapting to Different Personalities...

Understanding Personality Types:

Different people respond differently to persuasion. Adapt your approach based on whether the person is analytical, emotional, skeptical, or pragmatic.

Tailoring Your Communication Style:

For analytical types, use data and logic. For emotional types, focus on stories and emotional appeals. For skeptics, be prepared with solid evidence and case studies.

7. Moving Forward After Objections...

Finding a Middle Ground:

If there are still objections, try to find a compromise or a middle ground that satisfies both parties.

Agreeing to Disagree:

In some cases, it might be best to agree to disagree and revisit the conversation at a later time.

Actionable Next Steps:

End the conversation with actionable next steps, whether it's further research, another meeting, or a trial period.

8. Continuous Learning and Improvement…

Reflecting on the Conversation:

After navigating objections, take time to reflect on the conversation. What worked well? What could have been done differently?

Seeking Feedback:

If possible, get feedback from the other person or a third party. This can provide insights into your handling of objections.

Staying Informed and Updated:

Stay informed and updated on your topic. Being well-prepared can help you navigate objections more effectively.

Handling objections and challenges is an integral part of enrolling communication. By understanding and empathetically addressing concerns, maintaining a positive dialogue, and being adaptable to different personalities and situations, you can navigate these challenges effectively.

Remember, the goal is not to win an argument but to engage in a constructive dialogue that respects different viewpoints and leads to a mutually beneficial outcome.

CHAPTER VII

Influencing Others with "I'm Guessing You Haven't Got Around To..."

In the art of enrolling dialogue, the way we frame our words can significantly impact the listener's response. This chapter explores the strategic use of the phrase "I'm guessing you haven't got around to..." as a technique to guide someone gently towards a prior commitment that they have agreed. This phrase subtly nudges the listener to reconsider their actions without direct confrontation.

The Subtlety of Suggestion...

The phrase "I'm guessing you haven't got around to..." works on the principle of indirect suggestion. It presupposes that there is a task, idea, or change that the listener hasn't acted upon yet, but should have. This presumption can make the listener more open to considering what follows as a necessary action.

1. Presupposition:

This phrase cleverly uses presupposition suggesting that there is something the listener might have overlooked or delayed.

2. Non-confrontational Approach

By framing the language as a guess, the speaker avoids directly challenging the listener, which can reduce defensiveness and resistance. This framing also provides them an out as it reminds them of their prior commitment.

Section 1: Application in Various Contexts

The phrase "I'm guessing you haven't got around to…" has diverse applications in multiple contexts. Its efficacy lies in its gentle nudge towards action or reconsideration, making it a versatile tool in communication. This section explores its application in various settings, including business, personal relationships, and lifestyle changes.

In Business and Workplaces…

1. Introducing New Processes or Ideas

Scenario:

You are a team leader aiming to introduce a new software tool that you believe will improve efficiency.

Application:

"I'm guessing you haven't got around to exploring the new XYZ software. I think it could really streamline our project management and save us a lot of time."

Impact:

This approach brings the new tool to the team's attention in a non-confrontational way. It subtly suggests that overlooking this tool may be a missed opportunity, making the team more open to exploring it.

2. Addressing Procrastination in Projects

Scenario:

A project is lagging due to team members postponing tasks.

Application:

"I'm guessing you haven't got around to finalizing the report due next week. Would it be helpful to discuss how we can allocate resources to meet the deadline?"

Impact:

This phrase can gently push team members to acknowledge the delay and collaborate on finding a solution, avoiding direct blame.

In Personal Relationships and Family

3. Planning and Decision Making

Scenario:

Your family has been indecisive about planning a summer vacation.

Application:

"I'm guessing you haven't got around to looking at vacation spots yet. How about we sit down tonight and make a plan?"

Impact:

Here, the phrase is a soft prompt to start making concrete plans, steering the family from indecision to action.

4. Discussing Sensitive Topics

Scenario:

Needing to discuss a sensitive topic, such as finances or health, with a partner.

Application:

"I'm guessing you haven't got around to thinking about our retirement plan. It might be time we look into it together."

Impact:

The phrase can open up a conversation about sensitive topics in a non-threatening way, making it easier for partners to engage in the discussion.

In Health and Lifestyle Changes...

1. Adopting New Health Routine

Scenario:

Encouraging a friend to adopt a healthier lifestyle.

Application:

"I'm guessing you haven't got around to trying out that new health app I mentioned. It has some great features for tracking nutrition and exercise."

Impact:

This can encourage your friend to consider the health app without feeling judged or pressured, potentially leading to positive lifestyle changes.

2. Addressing Procrastination in Personal Goals

Scenario:

A friend has been postponing starting a new hobby or project.

Application:

"I'm guessing you haven't got around to starting your photography project. Maybe we can set aside some time this weekend to get it off the ground?"

Impact:

Such a nudge can motivate your friend to take the first step towards their hobby, offering support rather than criticism.

Professional Development & Career Advancement…

1. Encouraging Professional Growth

Scenario:

A colleague seems hesitant to take up a new training opportunity.

Application:

"I'm guessing you haven't got around to signing up for the advanced training course. I believe it could really boost your skill set for our line of work."

Impact:

Here, the phrase gently pushes the colleague to consider the training, highlighting its potential benefits for their career.

2. Navigating Career Transitions

Scenario:

Someone is considering a career change but is hesitant.

Application:

"I'm guessing you haven't got around to updating your resume for the job switch. How about we review it together?"

Impact:

This approach can provide the necessary push and support to someone contemplating a significant career move, making the process less daunting.

"I'm guessing you haven't got around to…" is an adaptable phrase that can be effectively used in a variety of contexts. Whether it's in a professional setting, within personal relationships, or in encouraging lifestyle changes, the phrase can gently guide conversations towards desired outcomes.

By tailoring its application to the specific context and audience, this phrase can be a valuable tool in facilitating action, decision-making, and open dialogue.

Section 2: Enhancing the Technique

The phrase "I'm guessing you haven't got around to…" is a subtle yet powerful tool in enrolling communication. However, its effectiveness largely depends on how it's delivered. This section delves into strategies to enhance this technique, ensuring that it is used to its fullest potential.

1. Building Rapport First

Importance of Connection...

Before using this phrase, establish a connection with your audience. Rapport creates a foundation of trust and makes the person more receptive to suggestions.

Techniques for Building Rapport...

Engage in small talk, show genuine interest in the other person's views, and mirror their body language subtly. This non-verbal mimicry can create a subconscious bond.

2. Tone and Delivery

Voice Modulation...

Use a tone that is curious and friendly. A harsh or condescending tone can make the phrase sound accusatory.

Pacing and Pausing...

Speak at a moderate pace and pause slightly before the phrase. This draws attention to what you're about to say and gives it more weight.

3. Customizing the Approach

Know Your Audience...

Tailor your approach based on who you are speaking to. What works for a colleague may not work for a friend or family member.

Contextual Awareness...

Be aware of the context in which you are using the phrase. The same words can have different implications in different situations.

4. Clarity and Precision

Being Specific...

Vague suggestions may not elicit a strong response. Be as specific as possible about what you are referring to.

Avoiding Ambiguity...

Ensure that your phrase is clear and does not leave room for misinterpretation.

5. Follow-Up Questions

Encouraging Dialogue...

After using the phrase, follow up with open-ended questions to encourage further discussion.

Active Listening...

Show that you are actively listening to their response. This will not only provide you with more information but also show respect for their viewpoint.

6. Handling Responses

Positive Reinforcement...

If the response is positive, reinforce it by showing enthusiasm and agreeing with their points.

Overcoming Negativity...

If the response is negative or defensive, don't counter-attack. Instead, try to understand the reason behind this reaction and address it calmly.

7. Combining with Enrolling Techniques

Anchoring...

Associate positive feelings or outcomes with the action you are suggesting. For instance, "I'm guessing you haven't got around to trying the new accounting software, which I've heard can drastically reduce workload."

Storytelling...

Use anecdotes or stories that highlight the benefits of the action you're suggesting. Stories can be a powerful way to convey your message.

8. Practice and Refinement

Regular Practice...

Regularly practice this phrase in different contexts to become more comfortable with its use.

Self-Reflection...

After each conversation, reflect on how well you used the phrase and what could be improved.

Seeking Feedback...

If possible, ask for feedback from the person you were conversing with or a third party.

9. Flexibility and Adaptability

Being Flexible...

Be prepared to change your approach based on the situation and the responses you receive.

Adapting to Objections...

If the person objects to your suggestion, don't insist. Instead, try to understand their perspective and adapt your suggestion accordingly.

10. Using the Technique Ethically

Respecting Boundaries...

Use this phrase ethically. Respect the other person's boundaries and do not use it to manipulate or coerce.

Empathetic Approach...

Always approach the conversation with empathy. Understand that the other person's reasons or hesitations are valid.

Enhancing the technique of using "I'm guessing you haven't got around to..." involves a combination of rapport building, careful tone and delivery, customization according to audience and context, and the ability to handle responses effectively.

When used skillfully and ethically, this phrase can open doors to meaningful conversations and positive outcomes. It is a testament to the power of subtlety and suggestion in enrolling communication.

Section 3: Practice Scenarios

Applying the phrase "I'm guessing you haven't got around to..." in different contexts is crucial for mastering its use in real-life situations. This section provides detailed practice scenarios across various environments, helping you refine your skills in deploying this phrase effectively.

Scenario 1: Workplace Project Deadline

Situation:

You're a project manager, and one of your team members, Alex, is consistently behind on his project deadlines.

Practice:

Approach Alex and say, "I'm guessing you haven't got around to finalizing the Jenkins report. Is there any obstacle you're facing that I can help with?" This opens up a dialogue to understand any underlying issues and offer support.

Reflection:

Post-conversation, reflect on Alex's response. Was he defensive, or did he open up about challenges he's facing? Consider how your approach might have influenced his response.

Scenario 2: Family Health Improvement

Situation:

Your family has been trying to adopt healthier eating habits, but you've noticed a lack of enthusiasm.

Practice:

During a family dinner, try, "I'm guessing you haven't got around to trying that new salad recipe I sent last week. How about we make it together this weekend?" This makes the suggestion a collaborative and fun activity rather than a chore.

Reflection:

Observe your family's reaction. Are they more receptive and willing to try new recipes? Reflect on how making health improvement a shared activity can boost enthusiasm.

Scenario 3: Educational Setting

Situation:

As a teacher, you notice a student, Sarah, struggling with a new concept but not seeking help.

Practice:

Approach Sarah and say, "I'm guessing you haven't got around to asking for help with the new algebra topic. Would a one-on-one session be helpful for you?" This gently encourages her to seek the help she needs without feeling singled out.

Reflection:

Consider Sarah's reaction. Does she seem relieved, embarrassed, or something else? Reflect on how different approaches can affect a student's willingness to accept help.

Scenario 4: Community Volunteer Work

Situation:

In your community, there's a need for volunteers for a local event, but response has been lukewarm.

Practice:

At the next community meeting, say, "I'm guessing you haven't got around to signing up for the community clean-up day. We really could use your expertise in organizing events." This not only invites participation but also acknowledges the individual's skills.

Reflection:

Analyze the community's response. Are more people signing up? Reflect on how personal recognition can be a powerful motivator for community involvement.

Scenario 5: Personal Fitness Goals

Situation:

Your friend has expressed a desire to get fit but keeps postponing gym sessions.

Practice:

While hanging out, say, "I'm guessing you haven't got around to starting your gym routine. How about we join a class together?" This offers support and makes the goal seem more achievable.

Reflection:

Observe your friend's reaction. Does this offer make them more likely to commit? Reflect on how companionship can influence motivation for personal goals.

Scenario 6: Team Collaboration

Situation:

As a team leader, you notice that collaboration within your team is lacking, affecting overall productivity.

Practice:

In a team meeting, say, "I'm guessing you haven't got around to using the collaboration tools we implemented. What features would you like to see that would make them more useful for you?" This invites feedback and shows you're open to suggestions.

Reflection:

Assess how the team responds. Are they providing constructive feedback? Reflect on the importance of involving team members in decision-making processes.

Scenario 7: Networking Event

Situation:

At a networking event, you want to encourage follow-up meetings with potential contacts.

Practice:

To a promising contact, say, "I'm guessing you haven't got around to looking into our services. Would a one-on-one meeting be beneficial to discuss potential collaboration?" This piques interest without being too forceful.

Reflection:

Consider the contact's response. Are they more inclined to arrange a meeting? Reflect on how a soft approach can be more effective in networking than a hard sell.

Scenario 8: Addressing Procrastination

Situation:

A colleague often delays starting important tasks, affecting team deadlines.

Practice:

Privately say, "I'm guessing you haven't got around to starting the budget analysis. Is there a particular aspect you're finding challenging?" This offers an opportunity to discuss and address any issues hindering progress.

Reflection:

Analyze their response and your approach's effectiveness. Reflect on how offering help can sometimes be more effective than direct confrontation in addressing procrastination.

In each scenario, "I'm guessing you haven't got around to…" can be a gentle yet effective nudge towards action. These practices aim to help you apply this phrase in a range of situations, enhancing your communication skills and ability to influence positively.

Reflecting on each scenario's outcome is key to understanding the impact of your approach and adapting it for greater effectiveness in future interactions.

Section 4: Overcoming Obstacles

In using the phrase "I'm guessing you haven't got around to…", it's inevitable to encounter various obstacles. These can range from outright resistance to subtle discomfort or avoidance. This section provides strategies for overcoming these obstacles, ensuring that your communication remains effective and productive.

1. Handling Resistance

Understanding the Source...

Resistance often stems from underlying fears, lack of understanding, or simply inertia. Begin by identifying the root cause of the resistance.

Empathetic Approach...

Respond to resistance with empathy. Acknowledge their feelings and concerns, and provide reassurance where possible.

Reframing Resistance...

Use reframing techniques to shift the perspective. For instance, if someone resists a new idea due to fear of change, highlight the benefits and opportunities that change can bring.

2. Dealing with Discomfort or Avoidance

Gentle Probing...

When you sense discomfort or avoidance, probe gently. Ask open-ended questions to encourage the person to open up about their apprehensions.

Creating a Safe Environment...

Ensure the individual feels safe and respected. This can make them more willing to engage in conversation.

Using Encouragement...

Sometimes, all that's needed is a bit of encouragement. Highlight their strengths and past successes to bolster their confidence.

3. Overcoming Misunderstandings

Clarifying Intentions...

If there's a misunderstanding about your intentions, clarify them. Be explicit that your goal is to explore possibilities or solutions collaboratively.

Providing Information...

Misunderstandings often arise from a lack of information. Provide clear, concise, and relevant information to clear up any misconceptions.

Active Listening...

Listen actively to their concerns or objections. This not only shows respect but also helps you to understand and address the source of the misunderstanding.

4. Navigating Indifference or Passivity

Stimulating Interest...

Indifference can be challenging to overcome. Try to connect the topic to something the person is interested in or show them how it directly impacts them.

Creating Urgency...

Sometimes, creating a sense of urgency can motivate action. Explain the consequences of inaction or the time-sensitive nature of the issue.

Involvement in Decision-Making...

Involve them in the decision-making process. This can make them feel more invested and less indifferent.

5. Addressing Fear of Change

Highlighting Benefits...

Focus on the benefits that the change can bring. People are more likely to embrace change if they see clear advantages.

Small Steps Approach...

Propose starting with small steps. This can make the change seem less daunting.

Support and Assurance...

Offer support and assurance throughout the process of change. Knowing they have support can alleviate fears.

6. Balancing Persistence with Flexibility

Knowing When to Persist...

Sometimes, persistence is necessary to overcome obstacles. However, it's important to recognize when to push and when to back off.

Flexibility in Approach...

Be flexible in your approach. If one method isn't working, be ready to try another.

Patience is Key...

Overcoming obstacles often requires patience. Be prepared to invest time in the process.

7. Using Positive Reinforcement

Reinforcing Positive Responses...

When you notice a positive response or a shift in attitude, reinforce it. Acknowledge and praise the willingness to consider or engage.

Building on Small Wins...

Celebrate small victories. This can build momentum and encourage further openness and cooperation.

8. Continuous Learning and Adaptation

Reflecting on Experiences...

After each interaction, reflect on what went well and what didn't. Use these insights to refine your approach.

Seeking Feedback...

If appropriate, ask for feedback from the person you were communicating with. This can provide valuable perspectives on your approach.

Adapting to Different Personalities...

Be aware that different personalities may require different approaches. Adapt your strategy to suit the individual's personality and communication style.

Overcoming obstacles when using "I'm guessing you haven't got around to…" requires a combination of empathy, understanding, persistence, and flexibility. By employing these strategies, you can navigate through resistance, discomfort, and other barriers effectively.

The key is to maintain respectful and open communication, adapt to feedback, and be patient in guiding the conversation towards a constructive outcome.

Section 5: Reflecting and Adapting

Reflecting on and adapting your communication approach is vital for mastering the art of persuasion, especially when using nuanced phrases like "I'm guessing you haven't got around to…". This section delves into the importance of self-reflection and adaptation in enhancing your persuasive communication skills.

1. The Art of Self-Reflection

Importance of Self-Reflection...

Reflecting on your interactions allows you to assess the effectiveness of your communication style and strategy. It helps in identifying areas for improvement.

Analyzing Responses...

After using the phrase, take time to analyze the responses you received. Did the conversation lead to a positive outcome? Were there any unexpected reactions?

Identifying Patterns...

Look for patterns in how people respond to your approach. Are there certain types of responses or situations where your approach is more effective?

2. Adapting to Feedback

Openness to Feedback...

Be open to feedback, both positive and negative. Constructive criticism can provide valuable insights into how your communication is perceived.

Asking for Feedback...

Don't hesitate to ask for feedback directly from those you communicate with. Their perspectives can offer a different angle on your approach.

Incorporating Feedback...

Use the feedback to make adjustments to your approach. This might involve tweaking your tone, timing, or the way you phrase your questions.

3. Adjusting to Different Audiences

Understanding Your Audience...

Different audiences may require different communication styles. What works for a colleague may not work for a family member or friend.

Tailoring Your Approach...

Adapt your approach based on the audience's background, preferences, and personality. This customization can make your communication more effective.

Cultural Sensitivity...

Be mindful of cultural differences in communication styles. What is considered persuasive in one culture might be seen as aggressive or intrusive in another.

4. Flexibility in Communication

The Need for Flexibility...

Being flexible in your communication allows you to navigate unexpected reactions or situations more effectively.

Changing Tactics...

If you notice that your approach is not working, be ready to change tactics. This could mean using a different phrase or changing the subject of conversation.

Embracing a Dynamic Approach...

Understand that effective communication is dynamic. It evolves based on the flow of conversation and the reactions of those involved.

5. Learning from Successes and Failures

Analyzing Successes...

Reflect on situations where your approach was successful. What factors contributed to the positive outcome?

Learning from Failures...

Equally important is learning from failures. If a conversation did not go as planned, consider what could have been done differently.

Continuous Improvement...

View each interaction as a learning opportunity. Aim for continuous improvement in your communication skills.

6. Developing Emotional Intelligence

Importance of Emotional Intelligence...

High emotional intelligence can significantly enhance your persuasive abilities. It involves understanding your emotions and those of others.

Reading Emotional Cues...

Pay attention to emotional cues during conversations. This can guide you in adjusting your approach in real-time.

Responding with Empathy...

Always respond with empathy. Understanding and acknowledging others' feelings can foster a more open and trusting communication environment.

7. Seeking External Resources

Utilizing Training and Resources...

Consider seeking external resources like communication workshops, books, or online courses to improve your skills.

Mentorship and Coaching...

A mentor or coach can provide personalized guidance and feedback on your communication style.

8. Practicing Consistently

Regular Practice...

Practice your communication skills regularly. This could be in professional settings, social situations, or through role-playing exercises.

Experimentation...

Don't be afraid to experiment with different approaches. Sometimes, the most effective communication strategies are discovered through trial and error.

9. Balancing Confidence with Humility

Confidence in Communication...

Be confident in your communication. Confidence can be persuasive in itself.

Maintaining Humility...

Balance your confidence with humility. Be willing to admit when you're wrong and be open to learning from others.

Reflecting on and adapting your communication approach is a continuous process. It involves analyzing your interactions, being open to feedback, understanding your audience, and being flexible in your approach.

By continually refining your skills and being mindful of emotional intelligence, you can effectively use "I'm guessing you haven't got around to…" to enroll and influence in a wide range of contexts.

Remember, the goal is not to manipulate but to engage in meaningful and productive dialogue.

CHAPTER VIII

Managing Arguments with "What If We Found A Way To..."

In this enlightening chapter, we delve into a transformative communication technique that opens new horizons in resolving arguments and fostering innovation. The phrase "What if we found a way to..." is not just a question; it is a key that unlocks the vast potential of collaborative problem-solving and creative thinking in any conversation.

Whether you're navigating a complex business negotiation, resolving a personal dispute, or engaging in a community dialogue, the art of enrollment is critical. This chapter introduces you to a subtle yet powerful tool that can dramatically alter the dynamics of any discussion, turning confrontational situations into opportunities for constructive, mutually beneficial outcomes.

Explanation of the Phrase's Power...

"What if we found a way to..." is a phrase that embodies the essence of collaborative innovation and shared problem-solving. Unlike traditional argumentative approaches that often lead to a deadlock, this phrase invites participants to jointly explore solutions, fostering a spirit of teamwork and creativity.

1. Fostering a Collaborative Mindset

The phrase inherently shifts the focus from individual positions to collective possibilities. It transforms the conversation from a zero-sum game to a collaborative venture where all parties can contribute to and benefit from the outcome.

By asking "what if," you're not just proposing an alternative; you're inviting others to join you in a journey of exploration and discovery. It's an invitation to think outside the box and envision innovative solutions.

2. Encouraging Creative Problem-Solving

"What if we found a way to..." serves as a catalyst for creative thinking. It nudges participants to look beyond the obvious and consider a range of possibilities, some of which might be unconventional yet highly effective.

This approach recognizes that the most impactful solutions often emerge from collective brainstorming, where diverse perspectives and ideas converge.

3. Building Consensus and Ownership

When you involve others in the process of finding solutions, it creates a sense of ownership and commitment to the outcome. People are more likely to support and engage with solutions they have had a hand in creating.

This phrase is particularly effective in situations where buy-in from multiple stakeholders is crucial for successful implementation.

In this chapter, we will explore various strategies and techniques for effectively using "What if we found a way to..." in different contexts. We will provide real-world examples, practical tips, and insights into how you can harness the power of this phrase to turn challenging situations into opportunities for collaborative success.

By the end of this chapter, you will have a new perspective on resolving conflicts and building consensus. You'll be equipped with a powerful tool that not only enhances your persuasive abilities but also contributes to a more cooperative and creative environment in both your personal and professional life.

Section 1 - Fostering a Collaborative Mindset

In today's increasingly interconnected world, fostering a collaborative mindset is more crucial than ever. The phrase "What if we found a way to..." is a pivotal tool in this pursuit, as it naturally steers conversations towards shared goals and mutual understanding. This section delves into how this phrase can be instrumental in nurturing a collaborative atmosphere, including practical examples from various scenarios.

The Essence of Collaborative Communication...

Collaboration isn't merely about working together; it's about thinking together, sharing visions, and co-creating solutions. When you introduce the phrase "What if we found a way to..." into a dialogue, you're essentially inviting others to join you in a creative and cooperative venture. This approach shifts the focus from individual agendas to collective problem-solving.

Example 1: Resolving Workplace Conflicts

Scenario:

In a marketing team, there's a conflict over choosing a strategy for a new campaign. Some team members prefer a traditional approach, while others advocate for a more innovative, digital-first strategy.

Application:

The team leader, noticing the growing divide, steps in and says, "What if we found a way to integrate both traditional and digital elements, playing to the strengths of each approach?"

Outcome:

This question immediately changes the dynamics of the meeting. Team members start brainstorming how elements of both strategies can be combined. A digital campaign with a traditional storytelling approach emerges as a consensus, satisfying both groups and leading to a successful campaign.

Analysis:

By suggesting a collaborative solution, the leader transformed a polarizing debate into a unified, creative brainstorming session. The phrase encouraged team members to step out of their entrenched positions and consider a hybrid approach.

Example 2: Enhancing Community Engagement

Scenario:

A local community is debating the use of a public space. Some residents want it to be a park, while others argue for a community center.

Application:

A community organizer proposes, "What if we found a way to design a multi-purpose space that functions both as a park and a community center?"

Outcome:

This idea sparks a new wave of discussion, focusing on how such a space could cater to the needs of all residents. The community starts working together with architects and planners, leading to the creation of a versatile community hub.

Analysis:

The organizer's use of "What if we found a way to..." shifted the conversation from a binary choice to a creative exploration of inclusive solutions. It opened the door for innovative thinking and collective decision-making.

Example 3: Improving Customer Service

Scenario:

A customer service team at a tech company is facing complaints about the complexity of their product.

Application:

During a team meeting, one member suggests, "What if we found a way to simplify our user interface while maintaining the advanced features our long-term customers value?"

Outcome:

The suggestion leads to a collaborative project involving both the customer service and product development teams. The result is an updated interface with an improved user experience for new customers and retained complexity for advanced users.

Analysis:

The team member's proposition encouraged a collaborative approach to problem-solving, aligning different departments towards a common goal. The phrase prompted a balance between user-friendliness and technical sophistication.

Building Blocks of a Collaborative Mindset...

To effectively foster a collaborative mindset using "What if we found a way to...", several key elements should be in place:

1. Empathy and Understanding

Begin with a genuine effort to understand the perspectives and needs of all parties involved. Empathy is the cornerstone of collaboration, as it paves the way for trust and open communication.

2. Active Listening:

Give everyone a chance to voice their opinions and concerns. Active listening not only gathers diverse viewpoints but also makes participants feel valued and heard, increasing their willingness to collaborate.

3. Encouraging Diverse Perspectives

Embrace the diversity of ideas and solutions. A collaborative mindset thrives on the richness of different perspectives, leading to more innovative and comprehensive solutions.

4. Building Trust

Trust is a critical component of collaboration. Ensure transparency in communication and follow through on commitments. Trust builds a safe environment for sharing ideas and taking collective risks.

5. Promoting Shared Goals

Highlight common objectives and the benefits of working together towards these goals. When individuals see the value in achieving shared outcomes, they are more likely to contribute constructively.

6. Cultivating a Safe and Open Environment

Create an atmosphere where everyone feels safe to express their ideas and concerns.

An open and non-judgmental environment encourages risk-taking and innovation, crucial for collaborative endeavors.

Section 2: Encouraging Creative Problem-Solving

The phrase "What if we found a way to..." is not just a catalyst for collaboration; it's a springboard for creative problem-solving. In this section, we'll explore how this powerful phrase can ignite imaginative thinking and lead to innovative solutions, using three practical examples from different realms – business, education, and community initiatives.

The Role of Creative Problem-Solving...

Creative problem-solving involves looking beyond conventional solutions to find unique and effective responses to challenges. It's about thinking outside the box and exploring possibilities that may not be immediately apparent. When you introduce "What if we found a way to..." into a conversation, you're opening a door to imaginative and unexplored avenues.

Example 1: Innovating in Business

Scenario:

A software company is struggling to increase user engagement with its product. Traditional marketing strategies haven't yielded the desired results.

Application:

During a brainstorming session, one team member proposes, "What if we found a way to integrate gamification elements into our software to boost user engagement?"

Outcome:

This suggestion leads the team to explore gamification, an approach they hadn't considered before. They develop a series of interactive challenges and rewards within the software. The result is a significant increase in user engagement and customer satisfaction.

Analysis:

The team member's proposition of "What if we found a way to..." steered the group towards a creative solution that addressed the core issue in an innovative way. By framing the challenge as an opportunity for creative thinking, the team was able to break free from conventional strategies and find a novel approach.

Example 2: Enhancing Education

Scenario:

A high school history teacher is facing declining interest in her classes. Students find the traditional teaching methods unengaging.

Application:

She asks herself, "What if we found a way to make history lessons more interactive and relevant to students' lives?"

Outcome:

This leads to the incorporation of role-playing activities where students reenact historical events and debates. Students become more engaged, and their understanding of historical contexts improves significantly.

Analysis:

By questioning the traditional approach and seeking a creative alternative, the teacher revitalized her teaching method. The phrase "What if we found a way to..." served as a personal prompt to rethink and innovate her teaching strategy, making history more accessible and interesting for her students.

Example 3: Community Problem-Solving

Scenario:

A local community is grappling with the issue of waste management. The existing systems are inefficient and environmentally unfriendly.

Application:

In a community meeting, a resident suggests, "What if we found a way to implement a community-wide composting and recycling program?"

Outcome:

The suggestion is well-received, and a committee is formed to explore the idea. Eventually, the community establishes a successful composting and recycling program, reducing waste and promoting environmental consciousness.

Analysis:

The resident's use of "What if we found a way to..." opened up a dialogue that led to a sustainable and community-driven solution. It encouraged the community to think creatively and collaboratively about a pressing environmental issue.

Strategies for Encouraging Creative Problem-Solving

1. Creating a Safe Space for Ideas

Encourage an environment where all ideas are welcomed and valued. This safety net is essential for people to share their innovative and sometimes unconventional ideas without fear of judgment.

2. Diverse Perspectives:

Involve individuals from different backgrounds and expertise. Diverse perspectives often lead to more creative solutions as they bring varied experiences and ways of thinking.

3. Encourage Questioning

Promote a culture where questioning the status quo is encouraged. Asking "Why?" and "What if?" drives deeper thinking and opens up new possibilities.

4. Combining Ideas

Sometimes, creative solutions emerge from the combination of different ideas. Encourage participants to build on each other's suggestions, leading to unique and comprehensive solutions.

5 . Visualizing Solutions

Use visual aids like mind maps, flowcharts, or prototypes to help conceptualize and explore ideas. Visualization can make abstract concepts more concrete and understandable.

6. Embracing Failure as a Learning Tool

Normalize the concept that not every idea will be successful, and that failure is a valuable part of the learning process. Encourage a mindset where failure is seen as a stepping stone to innovation, not an endpoint.

7. Iterative Development

Promote an iterative approach to problem-solving where ideas are continuously refined and tested. This approach encourages ongoing creativity and adjustment based on feedback and results.

8. Using Analogies and Metaphors

Encourage the use of analogies and metaphors to draw connections between seemingly unrelated concepts. This can lead to surprising insights and innovative solutions.

9. Time for Reflection and Brainstorming

Allocate dedicated time for reflection and brainstorming sessions. Unhurried and pressure-free environments are conducive to creative thinking.

10. Encourage Cross-Disciplinary Collaboration

Foster collaborations that cross traditional boundaries between disciplines. These collaborations can lead to the cross-pollination of ideas and innovative solutions.

Overcoming Barriers to Creative Problem-Solving...

Creative problem-solving can be hindered by various barriers, such as rigid thinking, fear of failure, and a lack of resources. Here's how to navigate these challenges:

1. Breaking Down Rigid Thinking

Challenge assumptions and encourage questioning the 'way things have always been done.' This helps break down barriers of rigid thinking and opens up new possibilities.

2. Creating a Culture of Risk-Taking

Develop a culture where taking calculated risks is celebrated, even if it doesn't always lead to success. This attitude encourages innovation and out-of-the-box thinking.

3. Resource Management

Be resourceful and look for ways to maximize available resources. Sometimes constraints can actually fuel creativity, as they force you to think differently.

The phrase "What if we found a way to..." is a powerful tool for sparking creative problem-solving. It encourages individuals and groups to step beyond traditional methods and explore innovative solutions.

Whether in a business, educational, or community setting, this approach fosters a culture of creativity, collaboration, and continuous learning.

As you apply this phrase in various contexts, remember that creativity thrives in environments where ideas are freely shared, diverse perspectives are valued, and failure is seen as part of the journey to success.

By fostering these conditions and embracing a mindset of exploration and innovation, you can unlock the full potential of creative problem-solving and achieve remarkable outcomes.

Section 3: Building Consensus and Ownership

The phrase "What if we found a way to..." is not only a gateway to innovative solutions but also a powerful tool for building consensus and fostering a sense of ownership among participants. This section delves into how this phrase can be effectively used to create a collaborative atmosphere where every participant feels invested in the outcome, supported by three practical examples from different contexts.

The Importance of Consensus and Ownership...

Building consensus is about finding common ground and agreement among diverse opinions, while ownership refers to the feeling of personal investment and responsibility towards an outcome or decision. Both are crucial for the success and sustainability of any initiative or solution. The phrase "What if we found a way to..." invites participation and input, naturally leading to a sense of shared ownership and consensus.

Example 1: Corporate Decision-Making

Scenario:

A corporate team is faced with the challenge of reducing operational costs without sacrificing employee satisfaction.

Application:

The manager introduces the idea, "What if we found a way to reduce costs through innovative methods that also enhance employee satisfaction?"

Outcome:

This leads to a series of brainstorming sessions where employees contribute various ideas, such as flexible working hours and green initiatives that reduce costs and benefit the workforce. The implementation of these ideas leads to a significant reduction in operational costs, along with an increase in employee morale.

Analysis:

By framing the cost-cutting challenge as a collaborative effort to improve the workplace, the manager created a platform where employees felt their input was valued. This approach not only built consensus around the decisions made but also ensured that employees felt a sense of ownership over the new initiatives.

Example 2: Community Development Project

Scenario:

A community is divided over the development of a new park. Some members want a children's playground, while others advocate for a community garden.

Application:

A community leader proposes, "What if we found a way to design the park to include both a playground and a community garden?"

Outcome:

The suggestion leads to community meetings where all members, including children, are invited to share their ideas. The final design includes both a playground and a community garden, meeting the needs of various community members.

Analysis:

The leader's use of "What if we found a way to..." encouraged inclusive participation, leading to a solution that reflected the community's diverse needs. This inclusive process fostered a strong sense of ownership among community members, ensuring the park's success and maintenance.

Example 3: Educational Curriculum Development

Scenario:

A school is struggling to develop a curriculum that is both academically rigorous and engaging for students.

Application:

The principal asks the faculty, "What if we found a way to develop a curriculum that balances academic rigor with engaging, student-centered learning?"

Outcome:

This question sparks a collaborative effort among teachers, students, and parents. The resulting curriculum includes project-based learning and interdisciplinary studies, making learning more engaging and effective.

Analysis:

By seeking input from all stakeholders, the principal ensured that the new curriculum was not only academically sound but also appealing to students. This collaborative approach led to a sense of shared ownership, with teachers and students feeling personally invested in the curriculum's success.

Strategies for Building Consensus and Ownership...

1. Inclusive Participation:

Ensure that all stakeholders have an opportunity to voice their opinions and ideas. Inclusivity fosters a sense of belonging and investment in the outcome.

2. Active Listening and Validation

Listen actively to all contributions and validate them. Acknowledging each participant's input encourages continued engagement and builds trust.

3. Transparency in Process

Be transparent about how decisions are made and how ideas will be incorporated. Transparency eliminates ambiguity and builds confidence in the process.

4. Facilitating Constructive Dialogue

Encourage respectful and constructive dialogue where differing opinions are discussed openly. This helps in finding common ground and forging consensus.

5. Highlighting Shared Goals

Emphasize the shared goals and objectives that everyone is working towards. Reminding participants of the common purpose helps in aligning diverse viewpoints.

6. Empowering Participants

Give participants roles and responsibilities in the decision-making process. This empowerment enhances their commitment to the project and its outcomes

7. Building Synergy

Facilitate interactions where participants can build on each other's ideas, creating a synergy that leads to more comprehensive solutions. This collaborative creation process further enhances the sense of ownership.

8.Providing Feedback Loops

Establish mechanisms for ongoing feedback throughout the process. This ensures that all voices are heard and considered, and adjustments can be made as needed.

9. Celebrating Contributions

Acknowledge and celebrate the contributions of all participants. Recognition fosters a positive atmosphere and encourages continued involvement and investment.

10. Focusing on Solutions, Not Personalities

Guide discussions to focus on ideas and solutions rather than personal opinions or egos. This helps maintain a constructive and objective tone in conversations.

Overcoming Challenges in Building Consensus...

Creating consensus and a sense of ownership among a diverse group can be challenging. Here's how to navigate common obstacles:

1. Managing Conflicting Interests

Recognize and address conflicting interests openly. Look for win-win scenarios where possible, and seek compromises that respect the concerns of all parties.

2. Dealing with Resistance

Understand the root causes of resistance. Engage with resistant individuals by seeking their input and addressing their concerns.

3. Maintaining Momentum

Keep the group motivated and focused, especially in long-term projects. Regular updates, milestone celebrations, and reminders of the end goal can help maintain momentum.

The phrase "What if we found a way to..." is a powerful tool for not only sparking creativity and collaboration but also for building consensus and a sense of ownership. By involving all relevant stakeholders in the process of finding solutions, and by ensuring that their voices are heard and valued, you create an environment where everyone is invested in the outcome. This approach leads to decisions that are more likely to be supported and implemented effectively.

Incorporating this approach in various contexts, whether in a corporate, community, or educational setting, can transform how decisions are made and how solutions are developed. It fosters a culture of collaboration, mutual respect, and shared responsibility, which are key ingredients for long-term success and sustainability.

As you apply "What if we found a way to..." in your interactions, remember that the goal is to create a space where consensus is valued and ownership is shared. This mindset not only leads to more effective solutions but also builds stronger, more cohesive teams and communities.

Section 4: Practical Scenarios and Training Exercises

In this section, we focus on applying "What if we found a way to..." in practical scenarios, offering a series of exercises and simulations designed to enhance your proficiency with this powerful communication tool. These activities are crafted to help you integrate this phrase into your daily interactions, improving your ability to foster collaboration, creativity, and consensus in various situations.

Practical Scenario 1: Workplace Collaboration

Situation:

Your team faces a challenging project with tight deadlines and differing opinions on how to proceed.

Exercise:

Conduct a role-playing activity where each team member presents their approach to the project. Then, reframe the discussion using "What if we found a way to..." to integrate the diverse ideas into a cohesive plan. Debrief by discussing how this approach changed the dynamics of the conversation.

Practical Scenario 2: Community Engagement

Situation:

You are part of a community meeting discussing the revitalization of a local park, with various conflicting interests from different community groups.

Exercise:

Break into small groups, each representing a different interest group. Use "What if we found a way to..." to propose solutions that address the concerns of all groups. Reconvene to share and evaluate the proposed solutions for their inclusivity and creativity.

Practical Scenario 3: Customer Service

Situation:

As a customer service representative, you're handling a call from a frustrated customer unhappy with a product or service.

Exercise:

Role-play the scenario with a colleague. Use "What if we found a way to..." to explore solutions that address the customer's concerns while also aligning with your company's policies. Discuss the effectiveness of this approach in diffusing the situation and reaching a satisfactory resolution.

Practical Scenario 4: Classroom Management

Situation:

As an educator, you are dealing with a class where students are disengaged with the current curriculum.

Exercise:

Invite students to a brainstorming session. Use "What if we found a way to..." to generate ideas for making the curriculum more engaging. Encourage students to think creatively and take ownership of their learning experience.

Practical Scenario 5: Personal Relationships

Situation:

You and your partner or family member have a disagreement about plans for a family vacation.

Exercise:

Use "What if we found a way to..." to openly discuss each person's preferences and concerns. Aim to find a solution that incorporates elements that everyone will enjoy. Reflect on how this approach impacts the quality of the conversation and the outcome.

Training Exercises

1. Daily Application Exercise

For one week, consciously use "What if we found a way to..." at least once a day in different contexts. Journal about the experience, noting changes in conversation dynamics and outcomes.

2. Group Brainstorming Sessions

Organize regular brainstorming sessions with your team or group where "What if we found a way to..." is used as a starting point. Discuss the effectiveness of this approach in generating diverse and innovative ideas.

3. Feedback Gathering

After using this phrase in various settings, seek feedback from others on how it influenced the conversation. Use this feedback to refine your approach.

4. Reflection and Adaptation

Reflect on the successes and challenges faced when using this phrase. Adapt your strategy based on these reflections to improve your effectiveness in different scenarios.

5. Conflict Resolution Role-Play

Engage in role-playing exercises where you simulate conflict scenarios. Practice using "What if we found a way to..." to navigate these conflicts towards constructive solutions.

6. Creative Thinking Workshops

Participate in or organize workshops focused on creative thinking and problem-solving. Use these workshops to practice applying the phrase in various brainstorming and innovation exercises.

7. Scenario Analysis

Analyze case studies or real-life scenarios where a lack of collaboration led to suboptimal outcomes. Discuss how using "What if we found a way to..." could have altered the course of these situations.

8. Peer Coaching Sessions

Pair up with a colleague or friend for regular coaching sessions. Take turns presenting challenges and using "What if we found a way to..." to explore potential solutions, providing feedback to each other.

9. Improvisation Activities

Engage in improvisational activities where participants must spontaneously respond to scenarios using "What if we found a way to..." This can enhance quick thinking and adaptability in using the phrase.

10. Mind Mapping

Utilize mind mapping techniques to visually organize thoughts and ideas generated from using "What if we found a way to..." This can help in seeing connections and developing comprehensive solutions.

Through these practical scenarios and training exercises, you can hone your skills in using "What if we found a way to..." effectively in various contexts.

The aim is to embed this phrase into your communication repertoire, making it a natural part of your dialogue in both personal and professional settings.

As you become more adept at using this phrase, you will likely notice a shift towards more collaborative, creative, and consensus-driven interactions.

Remember, the goal is not just to find immediate solutions but to cultivate an environment where open dialogue, innovative thinking, and shared ownership are the norm.

Section 5: Avoiding Common Pitfalls

While the phrase "What if we found a way to..." can be a powerful tool in promoting collaboration and creative problem-solving, there are common pitfalls that can diminish its effectiveness. This section addresses these potential issues and offers strategies to avoid them, ensuring that the phrase remains a potent and constructive part of your communication arsenal.

Pitfall 1: Overuse Leading to Ineffectiveness

The Problem...

If overused, "What if we found a way to..." can lose its impact, becoming a repetitive and predictable part of conversations that fails to inspire innovative thinking.

How to Avoid:

1. Use Judiciously

Reserve the phrase for situations where genuine collaboration and creative solutions are needed, rather than using it as a default response to every challenge.

2. Mix Up Your Language

Incorporate a variety of phrases to convey a similar sentiment. Alternatives like "How might we approach this differently?" or "Can we think of a solution that works for everyone?" keep the dialogue fresh and engaging.

Pitfall 2: Lack of Follow-Through

The Problem...

Suggesting "What if we found a way to..." raises expectations for action and change. Without follow-through, it can lead to disillusionment and a loss of credibility.

How to Avoid:

1. Set Actionable Plans

After using the phrase, immediately discuss and set concrete steps for implementation. Assign roles and deadlines to ensure accountability.

2. Track Progress

Regularly check in on the progress of the solutions derived from the phrase. This shows commitment to the ideas generated and maintains momentum.

Pitfall 3: Misalignment with Realistic Goals

The Problem...

Sometimes, "What if we found a way to..." can lead to suggestions that are not feasible or realistic, causing frustration and wasting valuable time.

How to Avoid:

1. Stay Grounded

Encourage creative thinking but within the realm of practicality. Solutions should be innovative yet achievable.

2. Assess Feasibility

Before diving into execution, evaluate the proposed ideas for their feasibility, resource requirements, and potential impact.

Pitfall 4: Ignoring Diverse Perspectives

The Problem...

The success of "What if we found a way to..." hinges on considering a diverse range of perspectives. Ignoring these can lead to biased or incomplete solutions.

How to Avoid:

1. Encourage Inclusivity

Actively seek input from all members of the group, especially those who might be quieter or less inclined to speak up.

2. Value Different Opinions

Show genuine interest in different viewpoints and encourage a culture where all ideas are respected and considered.

Pitfall 5: Creating a False Consensus

The Problem...

There's a risk of arriving at a superficial agreement that doesn't actually reflect the true consensus of the group, leading to issues down the line.

How to Avoid:

1. Encourage Open Discussion

Create a safe space for dissent and encourage constructive criticism. This helps ensure that any consensus reached is genuine and not just for the sake of agreement.

2. Check for Understanding

Periodically confirm that everyone is on the same page and that their concerns are addressed and integrated into the proposed solutions.

Pitfall 6: Misinterpreting the Intent

The Problem...

Sometimes, the intent behind "What if we found a way to..." might be misconstrued as avoidance of direct decision-making or as a lack of concrete ideas.

How to Avoid:

1. Clarify Purpose

Clearly communicate that the purpose of the phrase is to foster collaborative problem-solving and not to evade responsibility or decisions.

2. Combine with Direct Actions

Use the phrase in conjunction with clear actions and decisions. This demonstrates that it's part of a strategy towards effective problem-solving, not a substitute for it.

Pitfall 7: Inadequate Preparation

The Problem...

Without proper preparation or understanding of the context, using "What if we found a way to..." can lead to off-target suggestions and ineffective discussions.

How to Avoid:

1. Do Your Homework

Understand the context and background of the situation before introducing the phrase into the conversation.

2. Be Informed

Stay updated on relevant information, trends, and potential solutions to ensure that the discussions are productive and informed.

Pitfall 8: Dominating the Conversation

The Problem...

If one person or a small group dominates the conversation after posing "What if we found a way to...", it can stifle collaboration and limit the diversity of ideas.

How to Avoid:

1. Foster Equal Participation

Actively encourage input from all participants and moderate the discussion to prevent domination by a few voices.

2. Empower Others

Give everyone a chance to lead discussions or present their ideas, ensuring a balanced and inclusive conversation.

Pitfall 9: Failing to Build on Ideas

The Problem...

Merely suggesting "What if we found a way to..." without building on the ideas presented can lead to a lack of depth and progress in the conversation.

How to Avoid:

1. Encourage Idea Development

Prompt participants to expand on their ideas, and explore ways to combine and refine them for better outcomes.

2. Utilize Brainstorming Techniques

Employ methods like mind mapping or SWOT analysis to delve deeper into each suggestion and explore its potential.

Avoiding these common pitfalls is crucial in maximizing the effectiveness of "What if we found a way to..." as a tool for collaborative problem-solving and innovation.

By being mindful of these challenges and actively working to counteract them, you can harness the full potential of this phrase, leading to more productive discussions, inclusive decision-making, and creative solutions.

Remember, the goal is to use this phrase not just as a conversation starter but as a catalyst for meaningful change and progress.

234

CHAPTER IX

Weaving a Common Narritive with "This Reminds Me Of..."

This chapter focuses on the powerful role of shared experiences and memories in building connections and fostering understanding among people. We will dive into the psychological and social underpinnings of how relating personal experiences, anecdotes, or stories that start with "This reminds me of..." can create a mosaic of shared narratives, enhancing empathy and social cohesion.

The chapter begins by exploring the concept of narrative psychology and its significance in human interaction. It discusses how storytelling has been an integral part of human culture, serving not only as a means of entertainment but also as a tool for education and moral guidance. The phrase "This reminds me of..." acts as a bridge, linking individual experiences to collective memories, thereby creating a common ground for people from diverse backgrounds.

Subsequently, the chapter examines various contexts - from personal relationships to professional environments - where this narrative technique is employed. It presents case studies and real-life examples demonstrating how shared stories can break down barriers, build trust, and foster a sense of community. The role of empathy in this process is highlighted, showing how understanding and relating to others' experiences can lead to stronger, more meaningful connections.

Additionally, this chapter discusses the challenges and limitations of this approach, such as the potential for misunderstanding or the exclusion of those who cannot relate to the shared narrative. It offers guidance on how to navigate these challenges and use storytelling inclusively and effectively.

Overall, this provides a comprehensive exploration of how the simple act of sharing a story that begins with "This reminds me of…" can weave a rich, interconnected narrative fabric that strengthens social bonds and fosters a sense of belonging and understanding among people.

The Power of Relatability:

The phrase "This reminds me of…" works by connecting the current situation to something familiar to the listener. It taps into the human tendency to understand and interpret new information through the lens of past experiences or known narratives.

1. Creating a Connection

By linking to something familiar, you create a connection with your audience. This connection makes your argument more understandable and relatable.

2. Evoking Emotions

Often, the scenarios or stories you reference can evoke emotions, making your argument more impactful.

Section 1: Application in Various Contexts

The phrase "This reminds me of…" serves as a catalyst in various contexts, from personal relationships to professional settings. Its application transcends mere storytelling, becoming a tool for connection, understanding, and shared experience. In this section, we explore its utility in different scenarios, illustrating its power to weave a common narrative.

1. Personal Relationships

In personal relationships, "This reminds me of…" is often a gateway to sharing intimate memories and experiences. For example, when friends recount past adventures, each story, beginning with this phrase, not only recalls memories but also strengthens their bond. These shared narratives create a tapestry of mutual experiences, enhancing empathy and understanding. Importantly, this process allows individuals to see commonalities in their separate journeys, fostering deeper emotional connections.

An anecdote could illustrate this: Sarah and John, despite their different backgrounds, found a shared love for hiking. When Sarah mentioned a childhood hiking trip, starting with "This reminds me of…," John shared a similar experience. This exchange not only brought them closer but also helped them appreciate their diverse yet converging paths.

2. Professional Environments

In professional settings, "This reminds me of…" can be a powerful tool for team building and problem-solving. When team members share experiences or stories relevant to a work challenge, it can lead to innovative solutions. These shared narratives encourage a collaborative spirit, breaking down hierarchical barriers and fostering a sense of camaraderie.

Consider a scenario in a marketing team meeting. When faced with a difficult client, one member's anecdote, starting with "This reminds me of…," about a previous challenging project, can inspire a new approach or strategy. Such storytelling not only aids in problem-solving but also helps build a culture of shared knowledge and experience within the team.

3. Educational Settings

In education, "This reminds me of…" is more than a teaching technique; it's a bridge connecting theoretical knowledge with real-world experiences. Teachers and students alike use this phrase to relate academic concepts to personal experiences, making learning more relatable and engaging.

For instance, a history teacher discussing the Civil Rights Movement might share a personal story beginning with "This reminds me of…," perhaps about meeting a civil rights activist. This not only brings history to life for students but also encourages them to share their own related experiences or feelings, creating a more dynamic and interactive learning environment.

4. Therapeutic Contexts

Therapists often use "This reminds me of…" as a tool to help clients draw parallels between their experiences and broader human conditions. This technique can be particularly effective in group therapy, where individuals find comfort and understanding in shared experiences. It helps clients realize that their feelings and experiences, while unique, are also part of a larger human narrative.

For example, in a support group for grief, a member might start with "This reminds me of…" to share a moment of remembering a loved one. Such shared narratives can foster a supportive community, helping individuals feel less isolated in their grief.

5. Cultural Exchange

In cultural exchange, "This reminds me of…" is a powerful phrase for sharing and understanding different cultural narratives. It enables individuals from diverse backgrounds to find common ground in their unique cultural experiences. Through this, people develop a deeper appreciation and respect for different cultures, fostering a more inclusive and empathetic society.

Across various contexts, "This reminds me of…" is a versatile and powerful narrative tool. Whether it's strengthening personal bonds, fostering teamwork, enriching education, aiding therapy, or encouraging cultural exchange, this simple phrase unlocks the potential for deeper understanding and connection. By sharing and recognizing common narratives, we weave a tapestry of shared human experience, bridging gaps and building a more empathetic and connected world.

Section 2: Enhancing the Technique

This section explores enhancing the narrative technique of "This reminds me of…" through detailed subsections. Each of the following includes a Scenario, Application, Outcome, and Analysis, providing a comprehensive understanding of effectively utilizing this storytelling method.

1. Mindful Storytelling

Scenario:

In a team meeting, a manager faces low morale due to a recent project setback.

Application:

The manager begins with, "This reminds me of a time when…", sharing a past challenge and how it was overcome.

Outcome:

The team feels more motivated, realizing setbacks are part of the growth process.

Analysis:

This example shows the power of contextually relevant stories in inspiring and uniting a team, demonstrating empathetic leadership.

2. Active Listening and Engagement

Scenario:

A teacher discusses climate change, noticing students are disengaged.

Application:

The teacher shares a personal anecdote starting with "This reminds me of…", relating to a local environmental change and encourages student participation.

Outcome:

Students become more engaged, sharing their observations and concerns, leading to a lively discussion.

Analysis:

This scenario highlights the importance of active engagement in education, showing how personal stories can make complex topics more accessible and relatable.

3. Contextual Sensitivity

Scenario:

A therapist in a group session for anxiety sufferers.

Application:

The therapist uses "This reminds me of…" to share a generalized but relatable experience, careful not to dominate the conversation or minimize individual experiences.

Outcome:

Group members feel understood and more comfortable sharing their own stories.

Analysis:

The therapist's careful application of the phrase illustrates the need for sensitivity and relevance in therapeutic settings, enhancing mutual understanding and support.

4. Diversity and Inclusivity

Scenario:

In a multinational company, employees from diverse backgrounds feel disconnected.

Application:

During a team-building exercise, members are encouraged to share stories with "This reminds me of…", focusing on cultural experiences.

Outcome:

Increased understanding and appreciation of different cultures, fostering a more inclusive work environment.

Analysis:

This example demonstrates how inclusive storytelling can bridge cultural gaps, promoting a diverse yet unified workplace.

5. Reflective Practice and Continuous Learning

Scenario:

A professional development workshop for educators.

Application:

Participants are asked to share experiences with "This reminds me of…" regarding classroom challenges. Facilitators guide a reflective discussion on the outcomes.

Outcome:

Educators gain new perspectives and strategies for classroom management.

Analysis:

This scenario shows the importance of reflective practice in continuous learning, particularly in enhancing narrative skills for diverse applications.

Through these scenarios and their analyses, we see how the phrase "This reminds me of…" can be effectively employed in various contexts. Each example underscores the importance of mindful storytelling, active listening, contextual sensitivity, inclusivity, and reflective practice in creating meaningful narratives that resonate and foster deeper understanding.

Section 3: Practice Scenarios with Examples

This section provides practice scenarios with examples to demonstrate the effective application of "This reminds me of…" in various contexts. Each scenario is designed to illustrate how this narrative technique can be utilized to foster understanding, empathy, and connection among individuals.

Scenario 1: Bridging Cultural Gaps in the Workplace

Context:

A multinational corporation with a diverse workforce struggles with cultural misunderstandings.

Practice Scenario:

During a team-building session, employees are encouraged to share stories starting with "This reminds me of…" related to cultural traditions or holidays.

Example:

An employee from India starts with, "This reminds me of Diwali, the festival of lights in India…" and shares the significance of the festival and personal anecdotes. This prompts others to share similar stories about cultural festivals from their countries.

Outcome:

These shared narratives help colleagues understand and appreciate different cultural backgrounds, reducing misunderstandings and creating a more inclusive workplace.

Analysis:

The scenario demonstrates the effectiveness of shared storytelling in enhancing cultural understanding and empathy in a professional environment.

Scenario 2: Enhancing Classroom Engagement

Context:

A high school history class finds it difficult to relate to historical events.

Practice Scenario:

The teacher uses "This reminds me of…" to connect historical events to modern-day scenarios or personal stories.

Example:

While teaching about the Civil Rights Movement, the teacher shares, "This reminds me of a story my grandmother told me about her participation in a civil rights march…" This personal connection encourages students to share their thoughts and draw parallels with current events.

Outcome:

The students become more engaged and develop a deeper understanding of the historical events' relevance to the present.

Analysis:

This scenario highlights the role of personal narratives in making academic content relatable and stimulating student interest and participation.

Scenario 3: Conflict Resolution in Personal Relationships

Context:

A couple struggles with frequent misunderstandings and communication breakdowns.

Practice Scenario:

During a counseling session, they are encouraged to share experiences using "This reminds me of…" to express their feelings and perspectives.

Example:

One partner says, "This reminds me of when I felt unheard during our vacation planning…" and elaborates on their feelings. The other partner reciprocates with a similar narrative.

Outcome:

This approach allows each partner to express their emotions and experiences without direct accusation, leading to better understanding and conflict resolution.

Analysis:

The scenario shows how "This reminds me of…" can facilitate empathetic communication and understanding in personal relationships, aiding conflict resolution.

Scenario 4: Team Collaboration in Project Management

Context:

A project team faces challenges in collaboration and brainstorming creative solutions.

Practice Scenario:

The team leader initiates a meeting where each member shares a story starting with "This reminds me of…" related to past collaborative successes or failures.

Example:

A team member shares, "This reminds me of a time when a simple miscommunication led to a project delay..." and discusses the learning points. Others share similar experiences, leading to a discussion on effective communication and collaboration.

Outcome:

The session leads to a better understanding of past mistakes and successes, fostering a collaborative spirit and innovative problem-solving.

Analysis:

This scenario illustrates the use of shared narratives to enhance teamwork, communication, and creative problem-solving in a professional setting.

Scenario 5: Building Empathy in Healthcare

Context:

Healthcare professionals often struggle to understand patients' emotional and psychological experiences.

Practice Scenario:

In a training session, healthcare workers are encouraged to share patient stories with "This reminds me of...", focusing on empathy and understanding.

Example:

A nurse shares, "This reminds me of a patient who taught me the importance of listening…" and elaborates on the experience. This prompts others to reflect on similar experiences.

Outcome:

Such narratives help healthcare professionals gain insights into patients' perspectives, fostering empathy and improving patient care.

Analysis:

The scenario underscores the importance of narrative sharing in developing empathy and understanding in healthcare settings, which is crucial for patient-centered care.The practice scenarios and examples in this section illustrate the versatile applications of "This reminds me of…" across various contexts. Whether in resolving conflicts in personal relationships, enhancing collaboration in professional settings, making educational content more engaging, bridging cultural gaps, or fostering empathy in healthcare, this narrative technique proves invaluable.

By encouraging individuals to share personal stories and experiences, it opens avenues for deeper understanding, empathy, and connection. These scenarios serve as practical guides for effectively employing this technique in everyday situations, highlighting its power to transform interactions and relationships. As such, "This reminds me of…" is not just a phrase but a tool for building more cohesive, empathetic, and understanding communities.

Section 4: Avoiding Common Pitfalls

This section addresses the common pitfalls associated with using "This reminds me of…" in storytelling and communication. Understanding these potential missteps is crucial for anyone looking to effectively employ this narrative technique. By recognizing and avoiding these pitfalls, individuals can ensure their stories foster connection and understanding rather than inadvertently causing disconnect or discomfort.

1. Over-Dominance in Conversations

One of the primary pitfalls is allowing "This reminds me of…" to dominate conversations. While sharing personal stories is valuable, overuse can lead to monopolizing the conversation and not giving others the chance to contribute. This can occur in both personal and professional settings.

Example:

In a team meeting, if a leader consistently uses "This reminds me of…" to relate every discussion point to their own experiences, it may discourage team members from sharing their ideas or feelings. The leader's stories, while potentially valuable, can overshadow others' contributions.

Solution:

Balance is key. Use "This reminds me of…" sparingly and always encourage others to share their stories and perspectives. Active listening is as important as sharing.

2. Inappropriate or Irrelevant Stories

Another pitfall is sharing stories that are either inappropriate for the context or irrelevant to the discussion at hand. This can lead to discomfort among the audience or derail the conversation.

Example:

In a sensitive meeting discussing layoffs, an executive says, "This reminds me of the time I had to fire someone for the first time." Such a story could be perceived as insensitive and exacerbate an already tense situation.

Solution:

Always consider the context and the audience's feelings before sharing a story. Ensure that the narrative is relevant and adds value to the discussion.

3. Misjudging Cultural Sensitivities

In our increasingly globalized world, it's important to be aware of cultural sensitivities when sharing stories. A narrative that resonates in one culture may be misunderstood or offensive in another.

Example:

A manager in an international team meeting shares a story beginning with "This reminds me of..." that includes humor not universally understood or appreciated, leading to confusion or discomfort among team members from different cultural backgrounds.

Solution:

Cultivate cultural awareness and sensitivity. If unsure about how a story might be received, it's better to choose a more universally relatable narrative or ask for feedback from culturally diverse colleagues.

4. Undermining Personal Boundaries

Sharing personal stories can sometimes unintentionally infringe upon personal boundaries, making others uncomfortable or reluctant to engage.

Example:

During a team-building exercise, a person shares a deeply personal and emotional story starting with "This reminds me of…", which makes others in the group uncomfortable and hesitant to share their own stories.

Solution:

Respect personal boundaries and privacy, both your own and others'. Gauge the comfort level of the audience and adjust the depth and nature of the stories accordingly.

5. Neglecting the Opportunity for Dialogue

Finally, a common pitfall is not using "This reminds me of..." as an opportunity for dialogue. Sometimes individuals share their story and then move on without inviting others to respond or share their own experiences.

Example:

In a social gathering, someone shares a lengthy story starting with "This reminds me of..." but then quickly changes the subject, not allowing others to engage with the story or share their own.

Solution:

Encourage dialogue. After sharing a story, invite others to share their thoughts or related experiences. This fosters a two-way conversation and enriches the interaction.

Avoiding these common pitfalls is essential for effectively using "This reminds me of..." in communication. By being mindful of conversation balance, contextual appropriateness, cultural sensitivities, personal boundaries, and the importance of dialogue, individuals can ensure that their use of this narrative technique enhances understanding and connection. Remember, the goal is to weave a shared tapestry of stories that enrich and engage all participants, creating a more cohesive and empathetic community.

CHAPTER X

Navigating Adversity with Strategic Communication

Adversity is an inevitable part of human interaction, emerging in various aspects of our lives – from personal relationships and workplace dynamics to educational settings and community involvement. However, the way we approach and navigate these conflicts can significantly impact their resolution and the subsequent quality of our interactions and relationships. The intention is to equip readers with the tools and techniques necessary for effectively managing and resolving adversity through the power of strategic communication.

In this chapter, we delve into the art of combining specific phrases and communication strategies to transform potentially divisive situations into opportunities for understanding, growth, and collaboration. This approach is not just about finding the right words; it's about fostering an environment of empathy, open-mindedness, and constructive dialogue.

By understanding and applying these strategic combinations of phrases – such as "Imagine If", "Wouldn't It Be Great", and "I Understand Your Concerns, But Consider This" – individuals can open new avenues for resolution and find common ground even in the most challenging scenarios.

The chapter is structured to provide practical examples and scenarios across various contexts – from resolving marital and familial disputes to addressing workplace conflicts and facilitating positive changes in educational and community settings. Each section outlines specific phrase pairings and explains in detail why these phrases were chosen and how they can be assembled together to accomplish the desired outcome. This approach not only addresses the immediate conflict but also builds the skills necessary for effective communication in the long term.

Whether you are seeking to improve your personal relationships, enhance your professional interactions, or contribute positively to your community, this chapter offers valuable insights into the subtle art of conflict resolution through strategic communication. As you progress through each section, you will gain the tools to approach conflicts not as impasses but as stepping stones to deeper understanding and cooperation.

Section 1: Resolving Domestic Arguments

In this section we explore the art of resolving domestic arguments through the thoughtful pairing of persuasive phrases. By combining phrases like "Imagine If", "Wouldn't It Be Great", and others, we can facilitate more effective communication and conflict resolution in a domestic setting.

Each example demonstrates how specific pairings can be used to defuse tension, encourage understanding, and find common ground, with a detailed explanation of why these phrases were chosen and how they work together towards resolving arguments.

1. Creating a Vision for Harmony

Phrases:

"Imagine If" + *"Wouldn't It Be Great"*

Example:

"Imagine if we could resolve this argument peacefully. Wouldn't it be great to find a solution that works for both of us?"

Explanation:

These phrases help shift focus from the conflict to a harmonious vision, encouraging both parties to work towards a mutually beneficial outcome.

Desired Outcome:

To move away from confrontation and towards collaborative problem-solving.

2. Acknowledging and Redirecting Concerns

Phrases:

"I Understand Your Concerns, But Consider This" +
"What If We Found A Way To"

Example:

"I understand your concerns about spending too much, but consider this: What if we found a way to budget more effectively together?"

Explanation:

The first phrase acknowledges the partner's concerns, while the second suggests a practical solution, redirecting the conversation towards constructive problem-solving.

Desired Outcome:

To address the underlying issue and propose a solution.

3. Introducing External Perspectives

Phrases:

"I'm Not Sure If It's For You, But Maybe You Know Someone" + *"This Reminds Me Of"*

Example:

"I'm not sure if this approach is for you, but maybe you know someone who's tried it. This reminds me of our neighbors who successfully managed a similar issue."

Explanation:

This combination introduces an external example as a non-threatening way to suggest new approaches, making the idea more relatable.

Desired Outcome:

To offer new solutions without direct pressure.

4. Challenging Stagnation with Openness

Phrases:

"What's Stopping Us From" + *"How Open-Minded Would You Be"*

Example:

"What's stopping us from trying couples therapy? How open-minded would you be to attend just one session?"

Explanation:

The first phrase challenges current impasses, while the second encourages a willingness to try new solutions.

Desired Outcome:

To encourage considering new solutions to ongoing issues.

5. Addressing Delay in Responsibilities

Phrases:

"I'm Guessing You Haven't Got Around To" + "What If We Found A Way To"

Example:

"I'm guessing you haven't got around to fixing the leaky faucet. What if we found a way to schedule a time this weekend to work on it together?"

Explanation:

The first phrase gently brings up a delayed task, while the second offers a cooperative solution.

Desired Outcome:

To collaboratively address household responsibilities.

6. Fostering Empathy in Disagreements

Phrases:

"I Understand Your Concerns, But Consider This" +
"This Reminds Me Of"

Example:

"I understand your concerns about my work hours, but consider this: This reminds me of when you had to work late for your project last year."

Explanation:

Acknowledging the partner's concerns while relating it to a similar experience they had fosters empathy and mutual understanding.

Desired Outcome:

To build empathy and understanding.

7. Encouraging New Family Dynamics

Phrases:

"Imagine If" + "What's Stopping Us From"

Example:

"Imagine if we had more quality family time. What's stopping us from setting aside one evening a week for a family activity?"

Explanation:

The phrases create a positive vision and challenge existing barriers to family bonding.

Desired Outcome:

To encourage the establishment of new family traditions or routines.

8. Promoting Flexibility in Decision-Making

Phrases:

"How Open-Minded Would You Be" + "Wouldn't It Be Great"

Example:

"How open-minded would you be to trying a different approach to our holiday plans? Wouldn't it be great if we both enjoyed it more?"

Explanation:

The first phrase invites consideration of alternative options, while the second highlights the potential positive outcome of mutual enjoyment.

Desired Outcome:

To foster flexibility and compromise in planning and decision-making.

9. Reframing Perspectives on Shared Responsibilities

Phrases:

"I Understand Your Concerns, But Consider This" +
"What If We Found A Way To"

Example:

"I understand your concerns about being the only one doing the grocery shopping, but consider this: What if we found a way to make it a shared responsibility or more manageable for you?"

Explanation:

Acknowledging the issue while suggesting a collaborative solution encourages a sense of teamwork and shared responsibility.

Desired Outcome:

To address and redistribute household tasks more equitably.

10. Gently Addressing Sensitive Topics

Phrases:

"This Reminds Me Of" + *"I'm Guessing You Haven't Got Around To"*

Example:

"This reminds me of when we first talked about starting a family. I'm guessing we haven't got around to discussing it further. Should we set a time to talk about it?"

Explanation:

The first phrase gently brings up a previously discussed topic, while the second acknowledges potential hesitation or delay in revisiting the conversation.

Desired Outcome:

To open up a sensitive conversation in a non-confrontational way.

The strategic pairing of phrases in domestic arguments is an effective communication tool for resolving conflicts and enhancing mutual understanding.

By carefully choosing and combining phrases, individuals can address concerns, encourage empathy, and foster cooperative problem-solving.

These examples serve as practical strategies for individuals seeking to improve their communication skills within the household, promoting a more harmonious and supportive domestic environment.

Section 2: Addressing Workplace Conflict

In this section we explore resolving workplace conflicts through the thoughtful combination of persuasive phrases. Using phrases such as "What If We Found A Way To", "This Reminds Me Of", and others, we can facilitate effective communication and conflict resolution in professional settings.

Each example demonstrates how specific pairings can be employed to de-escalate tensions, encourage understanding, and foster collaborative problem-solving, with detailed explanations of why these phrases were chosen and how they work together to achieve resolution.

1. Encouraging Team Innovation

Phrases:

"Imagine If" + *"What If We Found A Way To"*

Example:

"Imagine if our team could lead this project to unprecedented success. What if we found a way to integrate everyone's ideas effectively?"

Explanation:

'Imagine If' sets a positive and ambitious tone, while 'What If We Found A Way To' invites collaborative problem-solving.

Desired Outcome:

To motivate the team towards innovative thinking and collaboration.

2. Balancing Validation with Forward Thinking

Phrases:

***"I Understand Your Concerns, But Consider This"* +
*"Wouldn't It Be Great"***

Example:

"I understand your concerns about the new workflow, but consider this: Wouldn't it be great if it saved us all a few hours each week?"

Explanation:

The first phrase acknowledges concerns, while the second redirects focus to potential positive outcomes.

Desired Outcome:

To address worries while highlighting the benefits of a new initiative.

3. Introducing New Perspectives

Phrases:

"I'm Not Sure If It's For You, But Maybe You Know Someone" + "This Reminds Me Of"

Example:

"I'm not sure if this strategy is for you, but maybe you know someone in your network who succeeded with it. This reminds me of a case study I read recently."

Explanation:

Introduces new ideas indirectly, making them less confrontational and more relatable through examples.

Desired Outcome:

To suggest new strategies or ideas in a non-threatening way.

4. Challenging Status Quo

Phrases:

"What's Stopping Us From" + "How Open-Minded Would You Be"

Example:

"What's stopping us from adopting this new software? How open-minded would you be to a trial period?"

Explanation:

The first phrase challenges existing limitations, while the second encourages openness to new solutions.

Desired Outcome:

To promote the adoption of new technologies or methods.

5. Tactfully Addressing Task Avoidance

Phrases:

"I'm Guessing You Haven't Got Around To" + *"What If We Found A Way To"*

Example:

"I'm guessing you haven't got around to finishing that report. What if we found a way to delegate some of your other tasks?"

Explanation:

The first phrase gently acknowledges a delay, while the second offers supportive solutions.

Desired Outcome:

To address unfinished tasks and provide support for completion.

6. Building Empathy in Disputes

Phrases:

"I Understand Your Concerns, But Consider This" +
"This Reminds Me Of"

Example:

"I understand your concerns about the deadline, but consider this: This reminds me of last year's project, where we faced similar challenges and succeeded."

Explanation:

Combines empathy with a reminder of past successes to inspire confidence and reduce anxiety.

Desired Outcome:

To alleviate concerns by referencing past achievements.

7. Fostering Team Cohesion

Phrases:

"Imagine If" + *"What's Stopping Us From"*

Example:

"Imagine if our team was known for its exceptional collaboration. What's stopping us from achieving that?"

Explanation:

Creates an aspirational vision for the team and challenges existing barriers to cohesion.

Desired Outcome:

To encourage teamwork and collective goal-setting.

8. Promoting Flexibility in Decision-Making

Phrases:

"How Open-Minded Would You Be" + *"Wouldn't It Be Great"*

Example:

"How open-minded would you be to revisiting our marketing strategy? Wouldn't it be great if we could increase our reach?"

Explanation:

Encourages openness to new ideas while highlighting the potential benefits.

Desired Outcome:

To stimulate reconsideration of existing strategies.

9. Addressing Workload Distribution

Phrases:

"I Understand Your Concerns, But Consider This" +
"What If We Found A Way To"

Example:

"I understand your concerns about being overwhelmed with work, but consider this: What if we found a way to redistribute tasks more evenly?"

Explanation:

Acknowledges the issue of workload while suggesting a practical solution.

Desired Outcome:

To address and solve issues of workload imbalance.

10. Introducing Change with Sensitivity

Phrases:

"This Reminds Me Of" + *"I'm Guessing You Haven't Got Around To"*

Example:

"This reminds me of when we first transitioned to remote work. I'm guessing you haven't got around to setting up your home office optimally. How can we assist?"

Explanation:

Relates current situation to past experience and gently addresses a potential oversight while offering support.

Desired Outcome:

To encourage adaptation to change with understanding and support.

Strategic phrase pairing is a crucial skill in resolving workplace conflicts. By combining phrases thoughtfully, individuals can defuse tension, promote understanding, and foster a collaborative atmosphere.

Each example demonstrates how to approach common workplace issues with tact, empathy, and forward-thinking, paving the way for more harmonious and productive professional environments.

Section 3: Reconciling Issues Between Teachers and School Administrators

In this section we explore resolving conflicts between teachers and school administrators through strategic phrase pairing.

The use of phrases such as "Imagine If", "Wouldn't It Be Great", and others can facilitate effective communication and conflict resolution in educational settings.

Each example demonstrates how specific pairings can be used to address misunderstandings, encourage collaborative problem-solving, and foster a positive educational environment, with detailed explanations of why these phrases were chosen and how they work together to achieve resolution.

1. Fostering a Collaborative School Environment

Phrases:

"Imagine If" + *"What If We Found A Way To"*

Example:

"Imagine if our school was the leading example of innovation in teaching. What if we found a way to integrate both our ideas to achieve this?"

Explanation:

'Imagine If' sets an ambitious goal, while 'What If We Found A Way To' suggests a collaborative approach to achieving it.

Desired Outcome:

To motivate both parties to work together towards a common goal.

2. Validating Concerns and Suggesting Alternatives

Phrases:

"I Understand Your Concerns, But Consider This" +
"Wouldn't It Be Great"

Example:

"I understand your concerns about our current assessment methods, but consider this: Wouldn't it be great if we could develop more engaging and effective ways to evaluate student learning?"

Explanation:

Acknowledges existing issues while redirecting the conversation towards constructive alternatives.

Desired Outcome:

To address concerns while exploring new possibilities.

3. Introducing New Perspectives in Decision-Making

Phrases:

"I'm Not Sure If It's For You, But Maybe You Know Someone" + "This Reminds Me Of"

Example:

"I'm not sure if this new curriculum approach is for you, but maybe you know a department that succeeded with it. This reminds me of a school that saw great improvements."

Explanation:

Introduces new ideas through external examples, making them less confrontational.

Desired Outcome:

To suggest new strategies or changes in a non-threatening way.

4. Challenging Existing Limitations

Phrases:

"What's Stopping Us From" + "How Open-Minded Would You Be"

Example:

"What's stopping us from implementing a more holistic student support system? How open-minded would you be to discussing this with the counseling team?"

Explanation:

Questions the status quo and invites openness to new ideas.

Desired Outcome:

To encourage consideration of innovative educational strategies.

5. Addressing Delay in Action

Phrases:

"I'm Guessing You Haven't Got Around To"* + *"What If We Found A Way To"

Example:

"I'm guessing you haven't got around to reviewing the new safety protocols. What if we found a way to go through them together?"

Explanation:

Gently brings up an uncompleted task while offering a collaborative approach to completing it.

Desired Outcome:

To facilitate completion of pending tasks.

6. Building Empathy in Discussions

Phrases:

"I Understand Your Concerns, But Consider This" +
"This Reminds Me Of"

Example:

"I understand your concerns about budget cuts, but consider this: This reminds me of when we creatively reallocated resources last year."

Explanation:

Combines understanding with a reminder of past successes to inspire confidence in facing current challenges.

Desired Outcome:

To alleviate concerns by referencing past problem-solving experiences.

7. Encouraging New Educational Initiatives

Phrases:

"Imagine If" + *"What's Stopping Us From"*

Example:

"Imagine if our school could offer more extracurricular activities for students. What's stopping us from seeking community partnerships to make this happen?"

Explanation:

Creates a vision for improvement and questions current barriers to achieving it.

Desired Outcome:

To inspire the implementation of new programs and activities that benefit students.

8. Promoting Flexibility in Policy Implementation

Phrases:

"How Open-Minded Would You Be" + *"Wouldn't It Be Great"*

Example:

"How open-minded would you be to revising our homework policy? Wouldn't it be great if we could reduce student stress while maintaining academic standards?"

Explanation:

Encourages consideration of policy changes while focusing on potential positive outcomes for students.

Desired Outcome:

To advocate for policy adjustments that benefit student well-being and learning.

9. Addressing Resource Allocation Concerns

Phrases:

"I Understand Your Concerns, But Consider This" + *"What If We Found A Way To"*

Example:

"I understand your concerns about the lack of classroom resources, but consider this: What if we found a way to apply for more grants or community donations?"

Explanation:

Acknowledges the problem while suggesting proactive solutions for resource acquisition.

Desired Outcome:

To find creative solutions for resource limitations.

10. Introducing Change with Consideration

Phrases:

"This Reminds Me Of" + "I'm Guessing You Haven't Got Around To"

Example:

"This reminds me of the time we updated our technology infrastructure. I'm guessing we haven't got around to training all staff on the new systems. How can we facilitate this?"

Explanation:

Relates to a past successful change and addresses a current need in a supportive way.

Desired Outcome:

To ensure smooth transitions and adequate training for new initiatives.

Strategic phrase pairing is essential in resolving conflicts between teachers and school administrators.

By thoughtfully combining phrases, educators and administrators can address misunderstandings, promote a collaborative atmosphere, and find constructive solutions to challenges.

Each example demonstrates how to navigate complex educational issues with tact, empathy, and forward-thinking, fostering a more positive and effective educational environment for both staff and students.

Section 4: Working Through Marital Issues

In this section we address resolving marital conflicts by skillfully combining persuasive phrases such as "Imagine If", "Wouldn't It Be Great", and others.

This technique facilitates effective communication and conflict resolution in a marital setting. Each example illustrates how these pairings can be used to ease tensions, encourage mutual understanding, and foster a stronger relationship, with detailed explanations of why these phrases were chosen and how they work together towards a positive outcome.

1. Envisioning a Harmonious Future Together

Phrases:

"Imagine If" + *"What If We Found A Way To"*

Example:

"Imagine if we could communicate without getting upset. What if we found a way to discuss our issues calmly and constructively?"

Explanation:

'Imagine If' helps envision a positive future, while 'What If We Found A Way To' suggests a practical approach to achieve it.

Desired Outcome:

To motivate both partners towards improving communication.

2. Acknowledging and Redirecting Concerns

Phrases:

"I Understand Your Concerns, But Consider This" +
"Wouldn't It Be Great"

Example:

"I understand your concerns about our finances, but consider this: Wouldn't it be great if we could work together on a budget that satisfies both of us?"

Explanation:

The first phrase shows empathy, while the second introduces a positive possibility.

Desired Outcome:

To address financial concerns while working towards a joint solution.

3. Introducing New Ideas Indirectly

Phrases:

"I'm Not Sure If It's For You, But Maybe You Know Someone" + *"This Reminds Me Of"*

Example:

"I'm not sure if marriage counseling is something you'd consider, but maybe you know someone who benefited from it. This reminds me of a couple who rekindled their relationship that way."

Explanation:

This approach introduces the idea of counseling in a non-confrontational way, using external examples.

Desired Outcome:

To suggest counseling or therapy without direct pressure.

4. Challenging the Status Quo

Phrases:

"What's Stopping Us From" + *"How Open-Minded Would You Be"*

Example:

"What's stopping us from spending more quality time together? How open-minded would you be to setting aside a date night each week?"

Explanation:

Encourages reevaluation of current routines and invites openness to new habits.

Desired Outcome:

To improve quality time spent together.

5. Tactfully Addressing Unfinished Business

Phrases:

"I'm Guessing You Haven't Got Around To" + *"What If We Found A Way To"*

Example:

"I'm guessing you haven't got around to fixing that leak. What if we found a way to work on it together this weekend?"

Explanation:

Addresses a delayed task in a non-confrontational manner and offers partnership in resolving it.

Desired Outcome:

To jointly tackle household responsibilities.

6. Building Understanding in Disagreements

Phrases:

"I Understand Your Concerns, But Consider This" +
"This Reminds Me Of"

Example:

"I understand your concerns about my long work hours, but consider this: This reminds me of when you were pursuing your degree and needed more time."

Explanation:

Acknowledges the partner's feelings while drawing a parallel to a similar past experience to foster empathy.

Desired Outcome:

To build mutual understanding and empathy.

7. Encouraging New Family Dynamics

Phrases:

"Imagine If" + *"What's Stopping Us From"*

Example:

"Imagine if we had a more peaceful and cooperative household. What's stopping us from implementing a family meeting each week to address our issues?"

Explanation:

Creates a vision for a harmonious family life and challenges existing barriers to this goal.

Desired Outcome:

To encourage the establishment of new family communication traditions.

8. Promoting Flexibility in Decision-Making

Phrases:

"How Open-Minded Would You Be" + "Wouldn't It Be Great"

Example:

"How open-minded would you be to try couples therapy? Wouldn't it be great if we could strengthen our relationship through it?"

Explanation:

Encourages consideration of new solutions while highlighting the potential benefits.

Desired Outcome:

To foster openness to seeking professional help for relationship improvement.

9. Addressing Concerns with Practical Solutions

Phrases:

"I Understand Your Concerns, But Consider This" +
"What If We Found A Way To"

Example:

"I understand your concerns about not spending enough time together. But consider this: What if we found a way to align our schedules better?"

Explanation:

Shows understanding of the partner's feelings and suggests a practical solution.

Desired Outcome:

To find effective ways to spend more quality time together.

10. Gently Bringing Up Sensitive Topics

Phrases:

"This Reminds Me Of" + *"I'm Guessing You Haven't Got Around To"*

Example:

"This reminds me of when we used to talk more openly about our feelings. I'm guessing we haven't got around to doing that recently. Shall we try again?"

Explanation:

Connects to a positive past experience and gently brings up the need to revisit open communication.

Desired Outcome:

To rekindle open and honest communication in the relationship.

Using strategic phrase pairing in marital communication is a powerful tool for resolving conflicts and building a stronger partnership.

These combinations facilitate understanding, empathy, and proactive problem-solving. Each example serves as a practical strategy for couples seeking to improve their communication skills and relationship dynamics, promoting a more harmonious and supportive marital environment.

Section 5: In Various Contexts

In this section we explore how strategic phrase pairing can be applied in diverse contexts, from personal relationships to professional environments. The combination of phrases like "Imagine If", "Wouldn't It Be Great", and others, is tailored to facilitate effective communication and achieve specific outcomes.

Each example demonstrates how pairing these phrases can address challenges, open up new possibilities, and encourage constructive dialogue, with detailed explanations of their selection and assembly.

1. Enhancing Team Collaboration in the Workplace

Phrases:

"What If We Found A Way To" + "Imagine If"

Example:

"What if we found a way to streamline our communication process? Imagine if this led to a 30% increase in team efficiency."

Explanation:

Proposes a practical solution and then uses visualization to highlight its potential impact.

Desired Outcome:

To motivate a team to adopt new communication strategies.

2. Encouraging a Friend to Pursue Opportunities

Phrases:

"I'm Not Sure If It's For You, But Maybe You Know Someone" + *"Wouldn't It Be Great"*

Example:

"I'm not sure if this job opportunity is for you, but maybe you know someone who would fit. Wouldn't it be great to help a friend find their dream job?"

Explanation:

Offers an opportunity in a low-pressure manner and underscores the joy of helping others.

Desired Outcome:

To encourage consideration of opportunities for oneself or others.

3. Facilitating Parent-Child Conversations

Phrases:

"I Understand Your Concerns, But Consider This" +
"This Reminds Me Of"

Example:

"I understand your concerns about going to a new school, but consider this: This reminds me of when I started at a new place and made my best friends."

Explanation:

Acknowledges the child's worries and shares a personal relatable experience to ease anxiety.

Desired Outcome:

To comfort and encourage a child facing a new situation.

4. Addressing Community Issues

Phrases:

"What's Stopping Us From" + *"How Open-Minded Would You Be"*

Example:

"What's stopping us from organizing a neighborhood clean-up? How open-minded would you be to participating?"

Explanation:

Challenges the status quo and encourages community members to consider involvement.

Desired Outcome:

To foster community engagement and action.

5. Encouraging Healthier Lifestyle Choices

Phrases:

"Imagine If" + *"What If We Found A Way To"*

Example:

"Imagine if we could both feel more energetic and healthier. What if we found a way to start a weekly exercise routine together?"

Explanation:

Creates a vision of improved well-being and suggests a collaborative approach to achieving it.

Desired Outcome:

To motivate a partner or friend to adopt healthier habits.

6. Facilitating Change in Organizational Policies

Phrases:

"I Understand Your Concerns, But Consider This" +
"Wouldn't It Be Great"

Example:

"I understand your concerns about changing our work-from-home policy, but consider this: Wouldn't it be great if our staff had more flexibility and work-life balance?"

Explanation:

Acknowledges hesitations about policy changes while highlighting potential benefits.

Desired Outcome:

To persuade decision-makers to consider more flexible policies.

7. Overcoming Procrastination

Phrases:

"I'm Guessing You Haven't Got Around To" + "How Open-Minded Would You Be"

Example:

"I'm guessing you haven't got around to starting your book. How open-minded would you be to setting aside 30 minutes each day for writing?"

Explanation:

Gently points out procrastination and proposes a manageable action plan.

Desired Outcome:

To encourage starting a long-postponed project.

8. Resolving Misunderstandings in Relationships

Phrases:

"This Reminds Me Of" + *"What's Stopping Us From"*

Example:

"This reminds me of our last misunderstanding. What's stopping us from setting clearer communication rules to avoid this in the future?"

Explanation:

Relates to a past issue and questions what can be done to prevent future ones.

Desired Outcome:

To improve communication in a relationship.

9. Encouraging Environmental Awareness

Phrases:

"Wouldn't It Be Great" + *"Imagine If"*

Example:

"Wouldn't it be great if our city had less pollution? Imagine if more of us chose to cycle to work."

Explanation:

Highlights a desirable outcome and uses visualization to promote environmentally friendly actions.

Desired Outcome:

To inspire more sustainable transportation choices.

10. Promoting Personal Development

Phrases:

"What If We Found A Way To" + "I'm Guessing You Haven't Got Around To"

Example:

"What if we found a way to learn a new language together? I'm guessing you haven't got around to starting those Spanish lessons you mentioned."

Explanation:

Suggests a joint venture in learning and gently nudges towards action on a previously expressed interest.

Desired Outcome:

To encourage the start of a new personal development activity.

Strategic phrase pairing is a versatile communication tool applicable in a wide range of scenarios. By carefully selecting and combining phrases, individuals can effectively address challenges, open up new possibilities, and encourage constructive dialogues in various aspects of life.

These examples serve as a guide to utilizing language to achieve specific goals, improve interactions, and foster positive change in personal, professional, and community contexts.